Dr. Nev's
Anabella
Giggles All Night!

Dr. Nev Nickelz   Mariah Grace
Author ★ Illustrator

Washington Longfellow Press

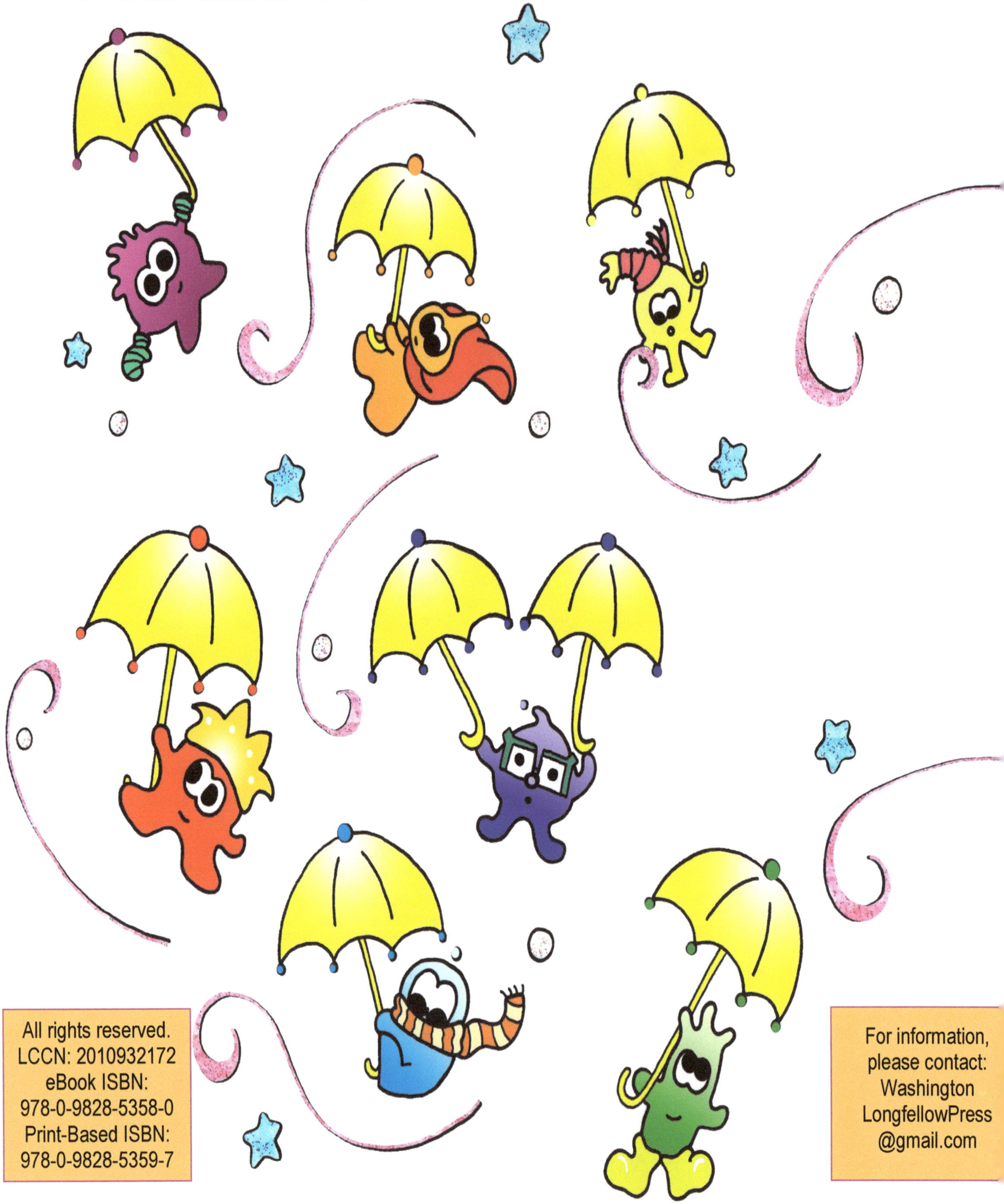

LCCN: 2010932172
eBook ISBN:
978-0-9828-5358-0
Print-Based ISBN:
978-0-9828-5359-7

For information,
please contact:
Washington
LongfellowPress
@gmail.com

Dr. Nev's Anabella Giggles All Night!

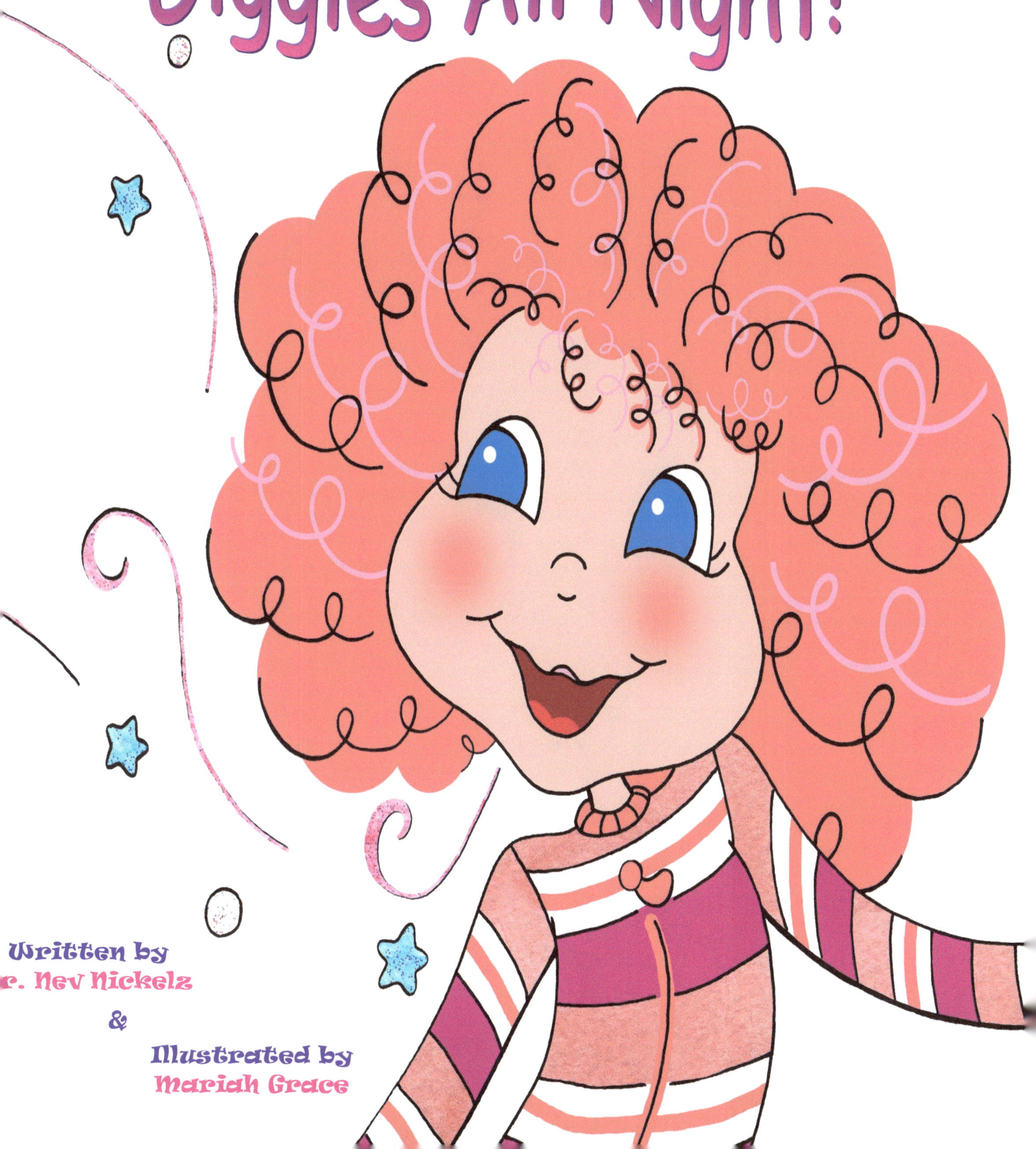

Written by
r. Nev Nickelz
&
Illustrated by
Mariah Grace

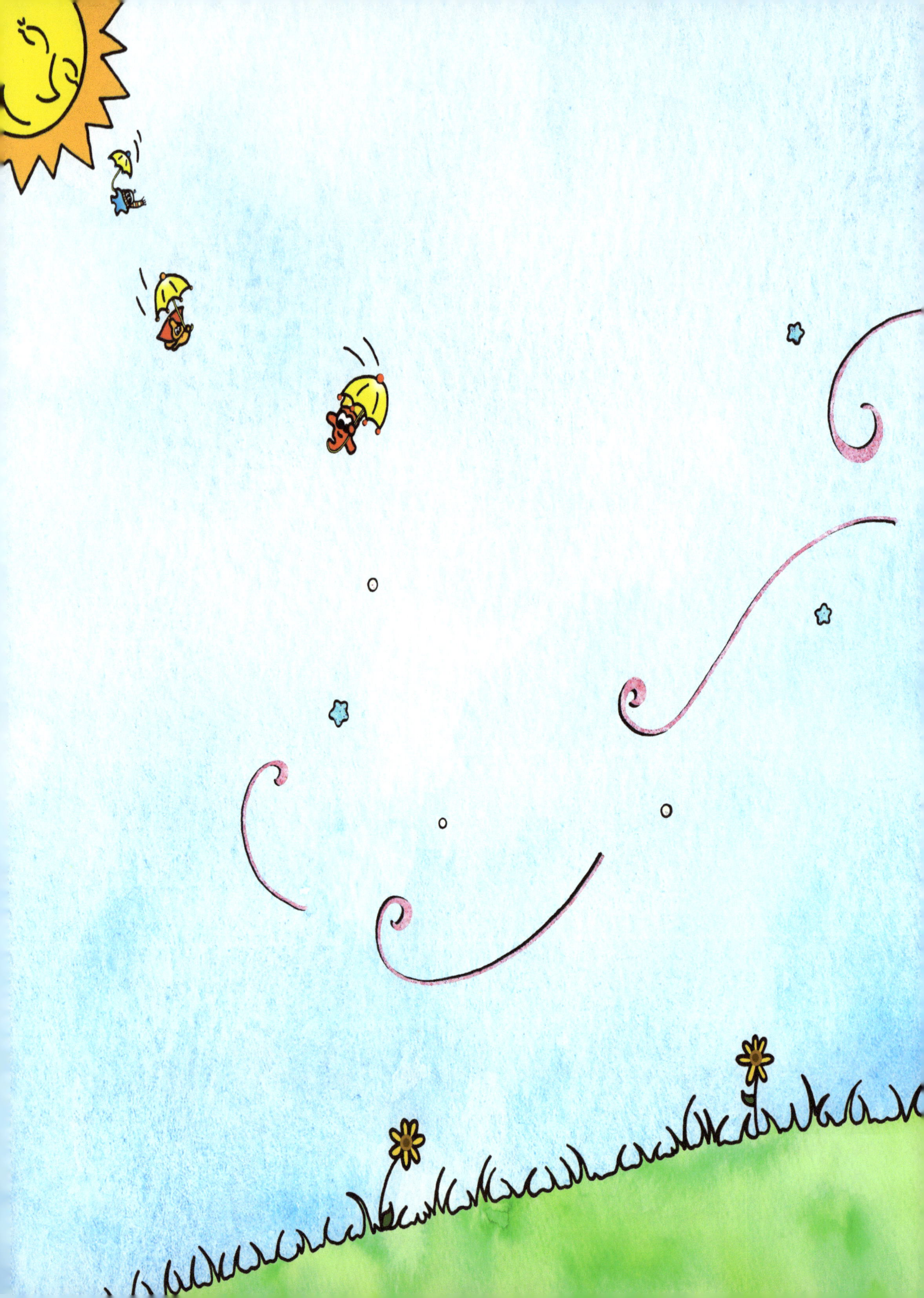

One sunny day,
Anabella declared
"I love to giggle!",
and her giggles filled up the air.

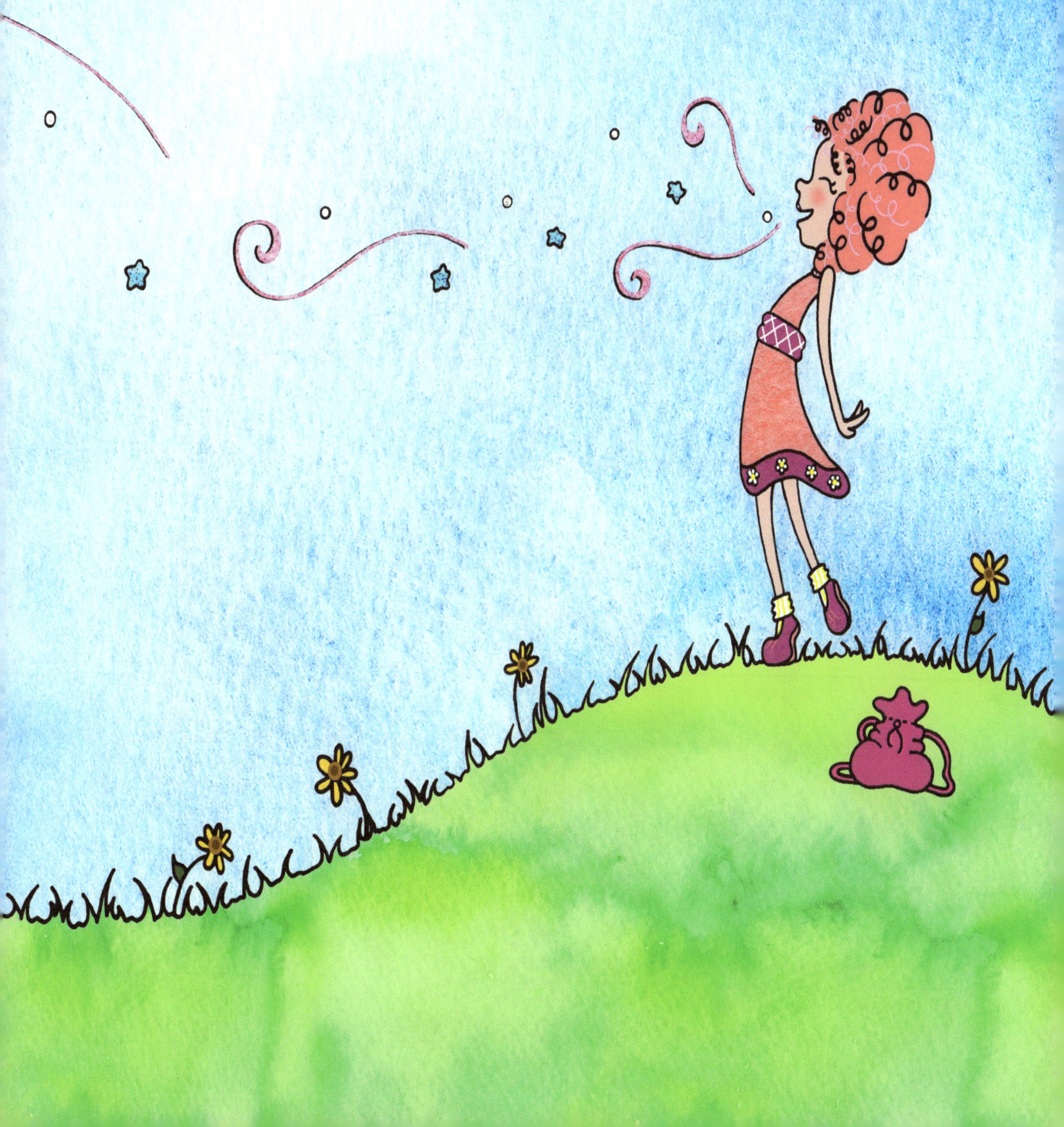

"Anabella" her teacher said
"I can't figure it out.
What is all
that giggling about?"

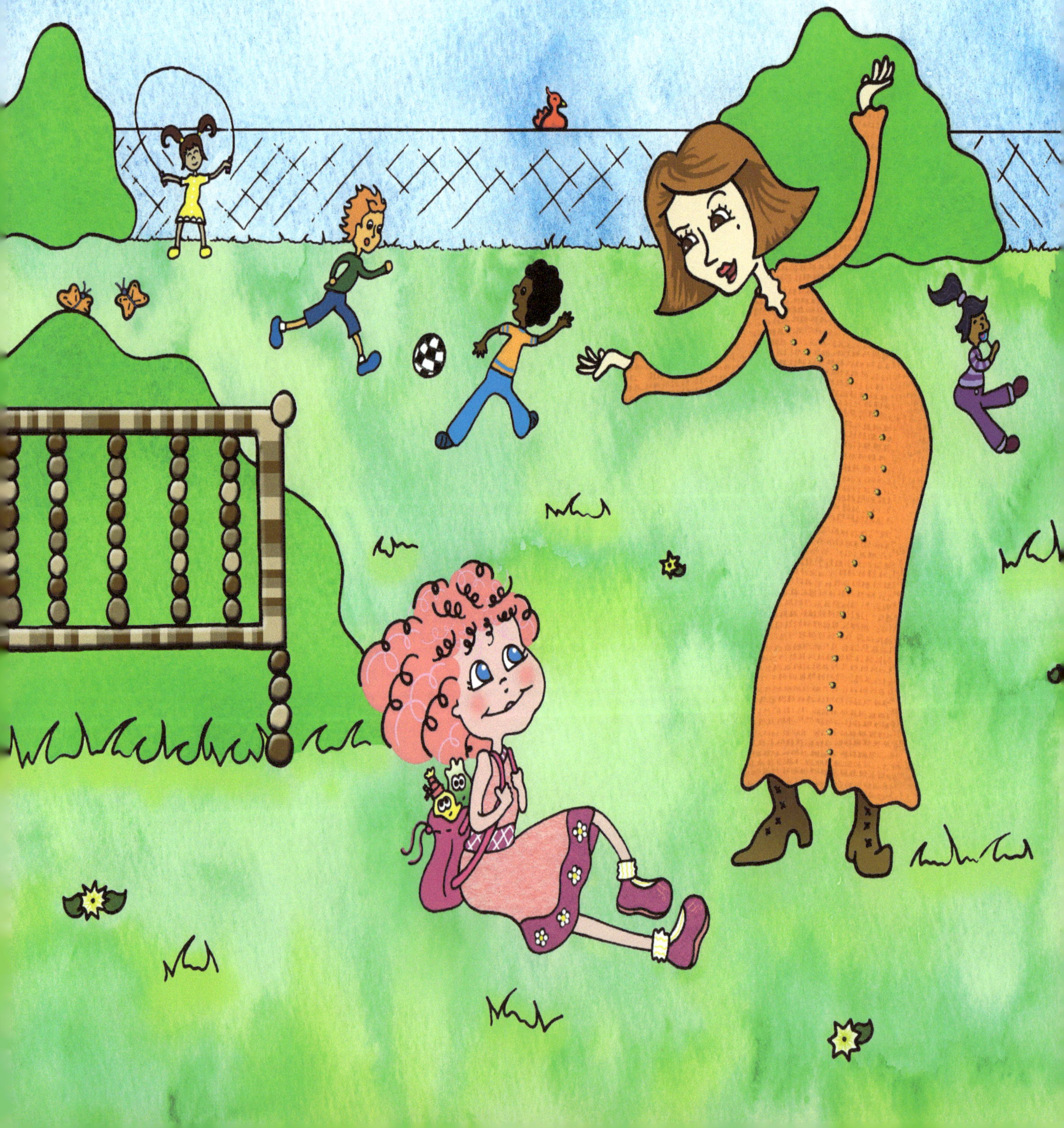

"Do you think you can
stop giggling for a little while?
Instead of more giggling,
can you make a pretty smile?"

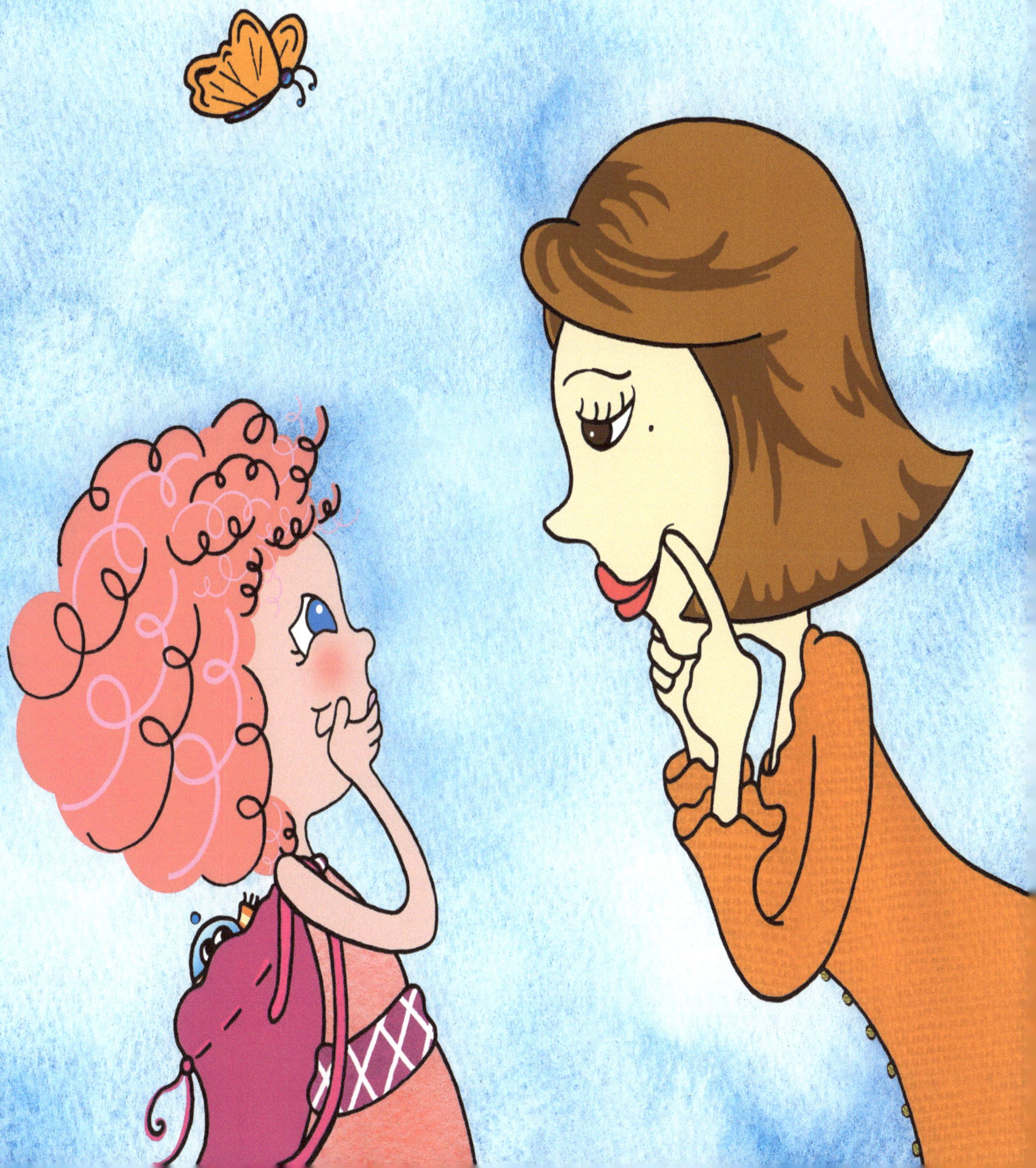

Anabella's mouth began
to move all around.

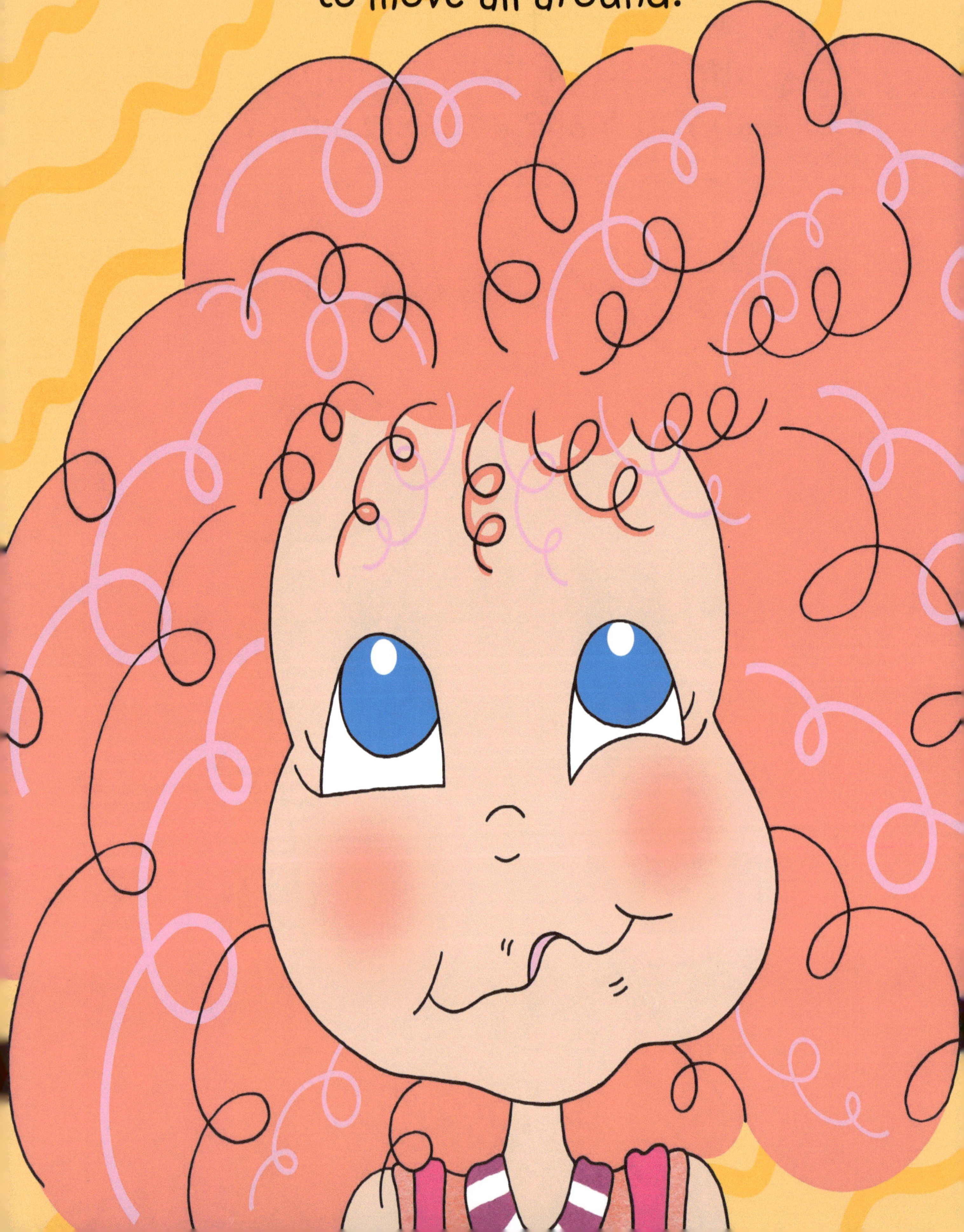

It made funny shapes,

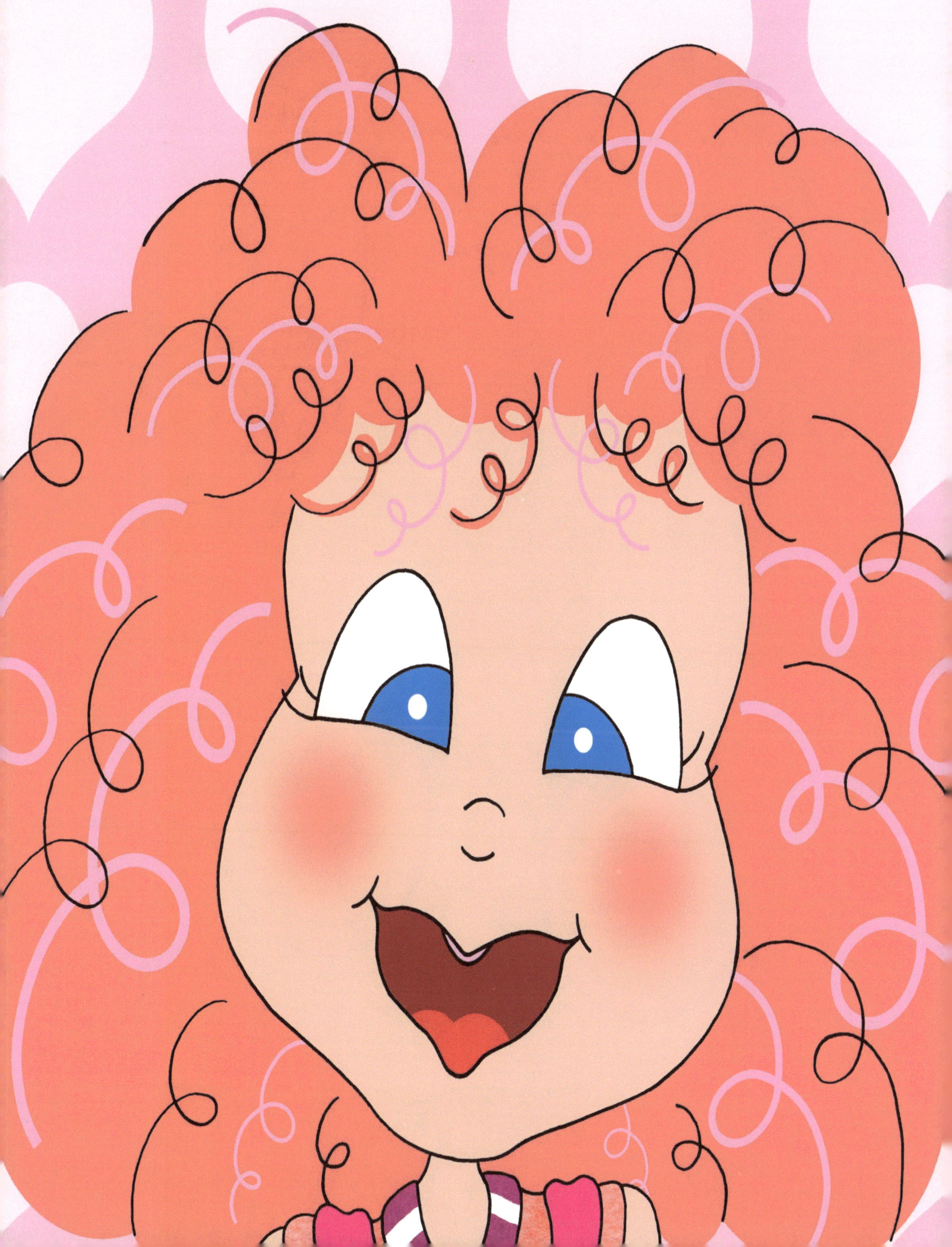

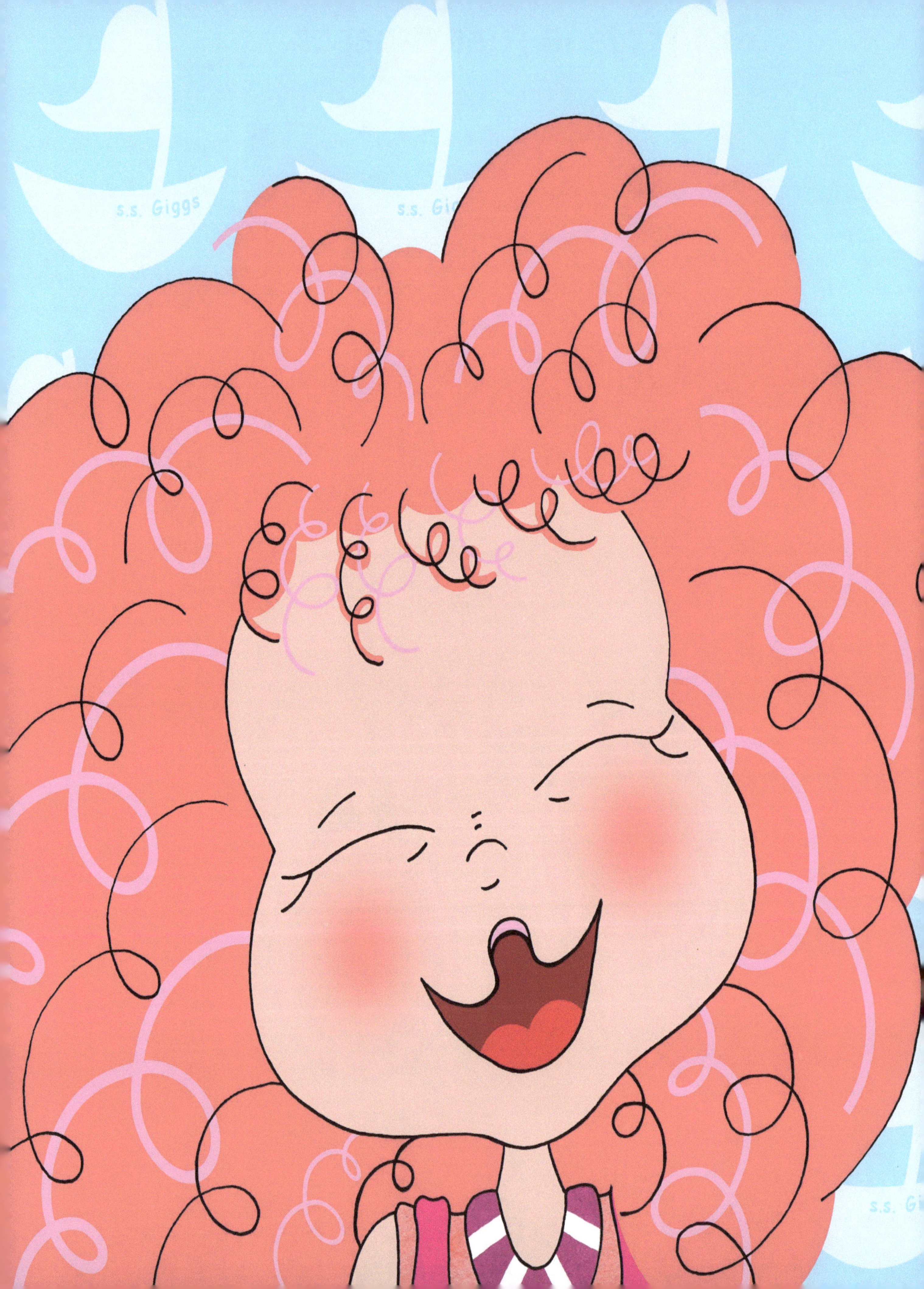
s.s. Giggs

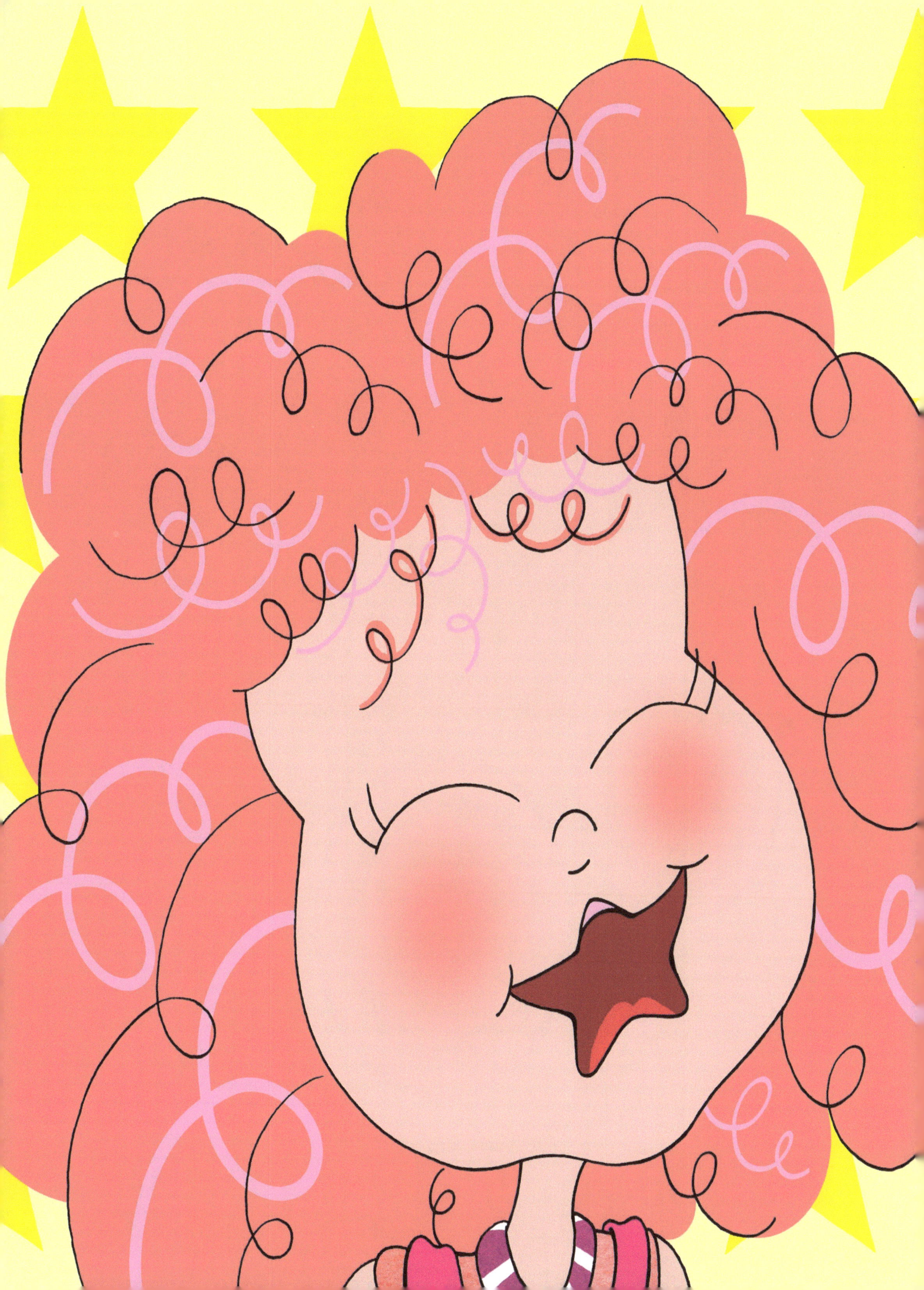

but did not make a sound.

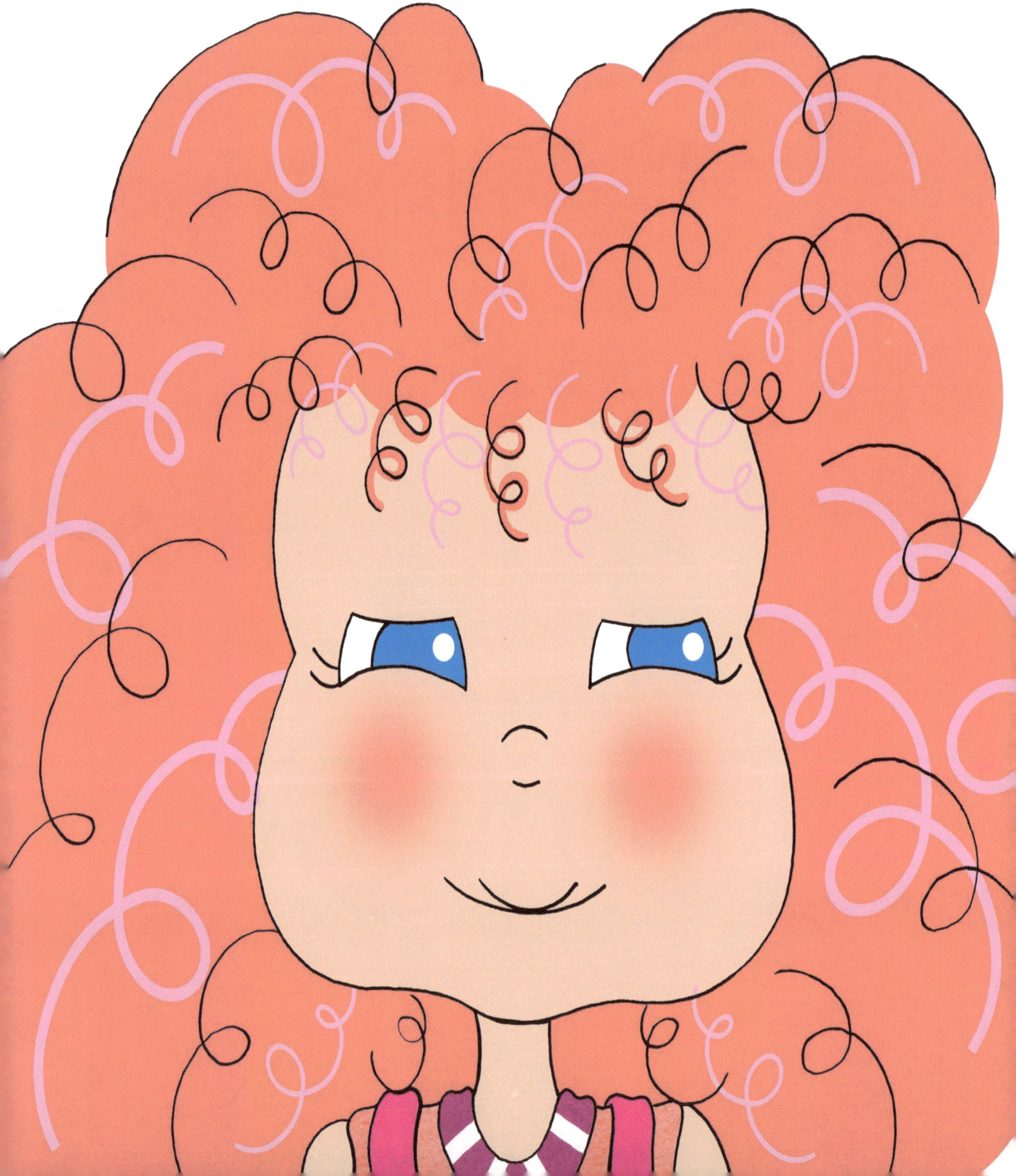

Then, it began to twitch mightily,

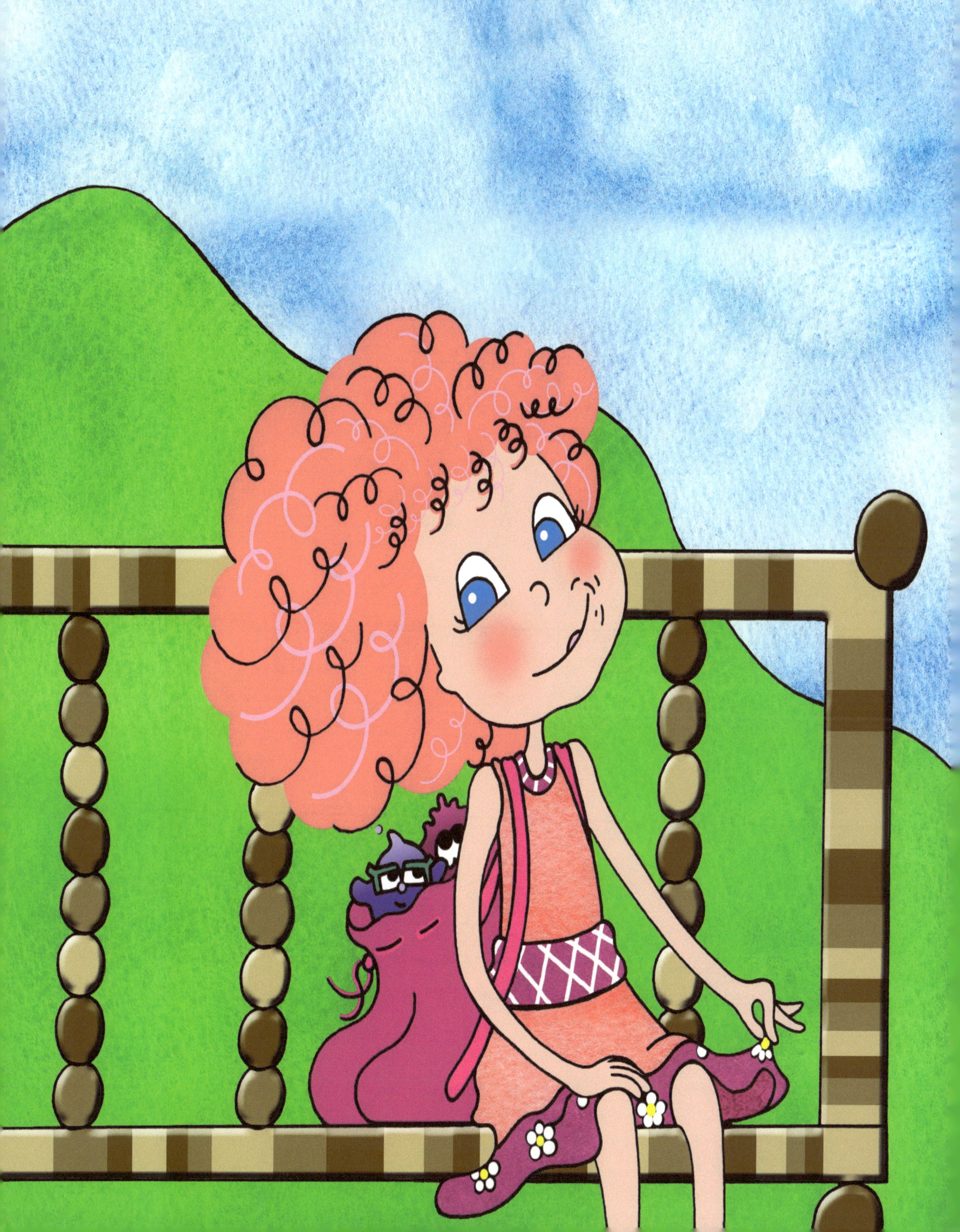

and her body started to shake most excitedly,

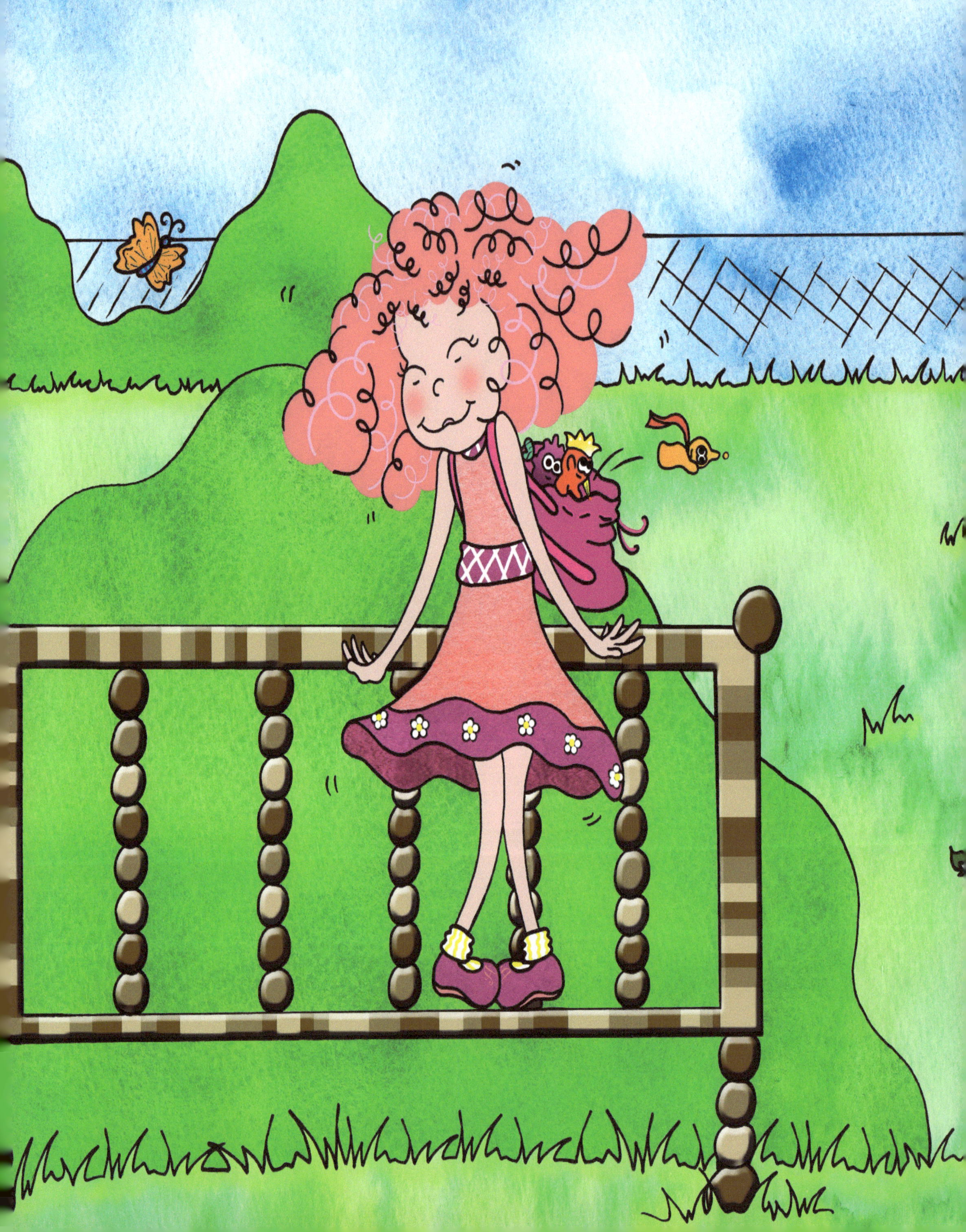

and out came those giggles,
as loud as can be!

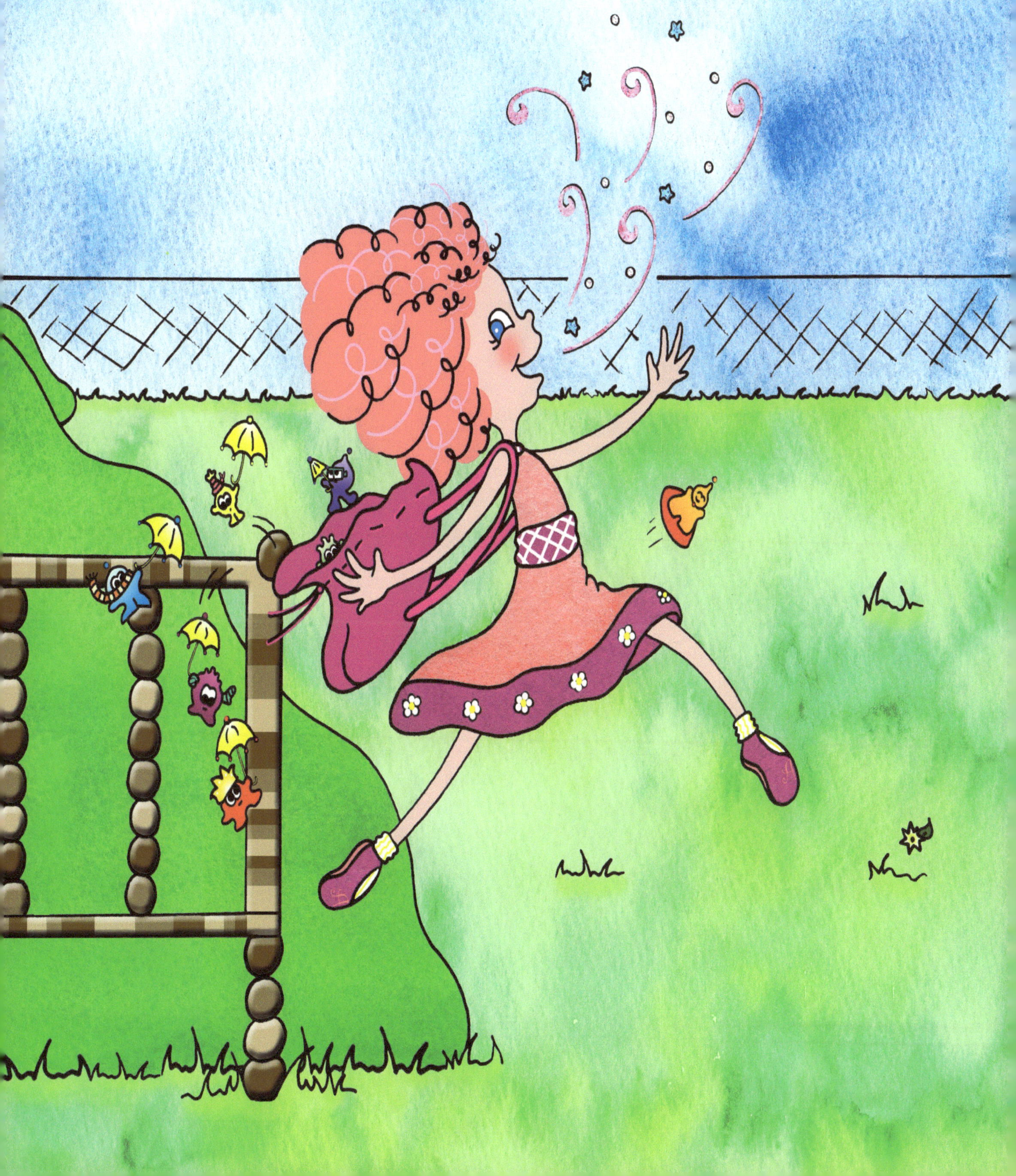

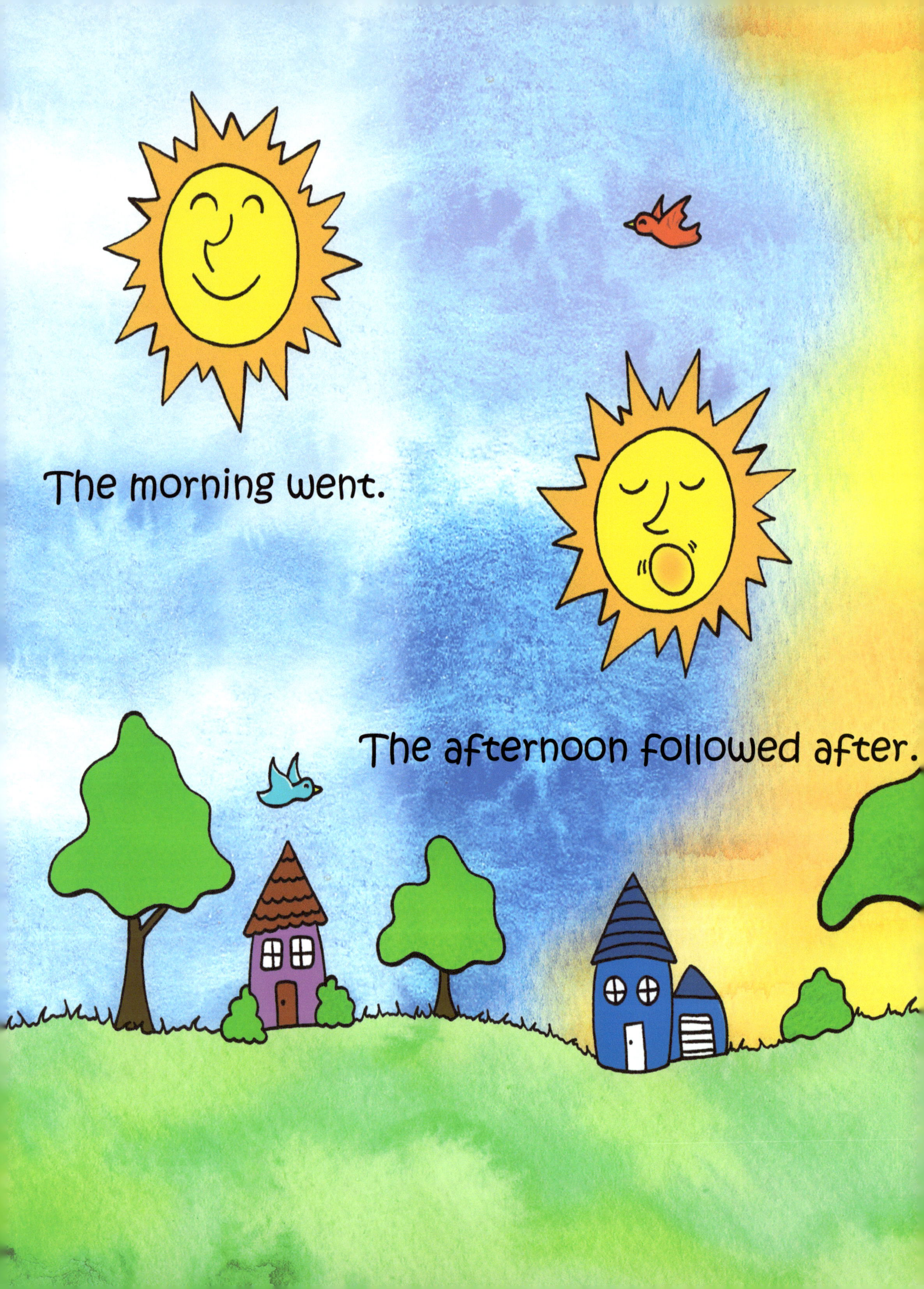

The morning went.

The afternoon followed after.

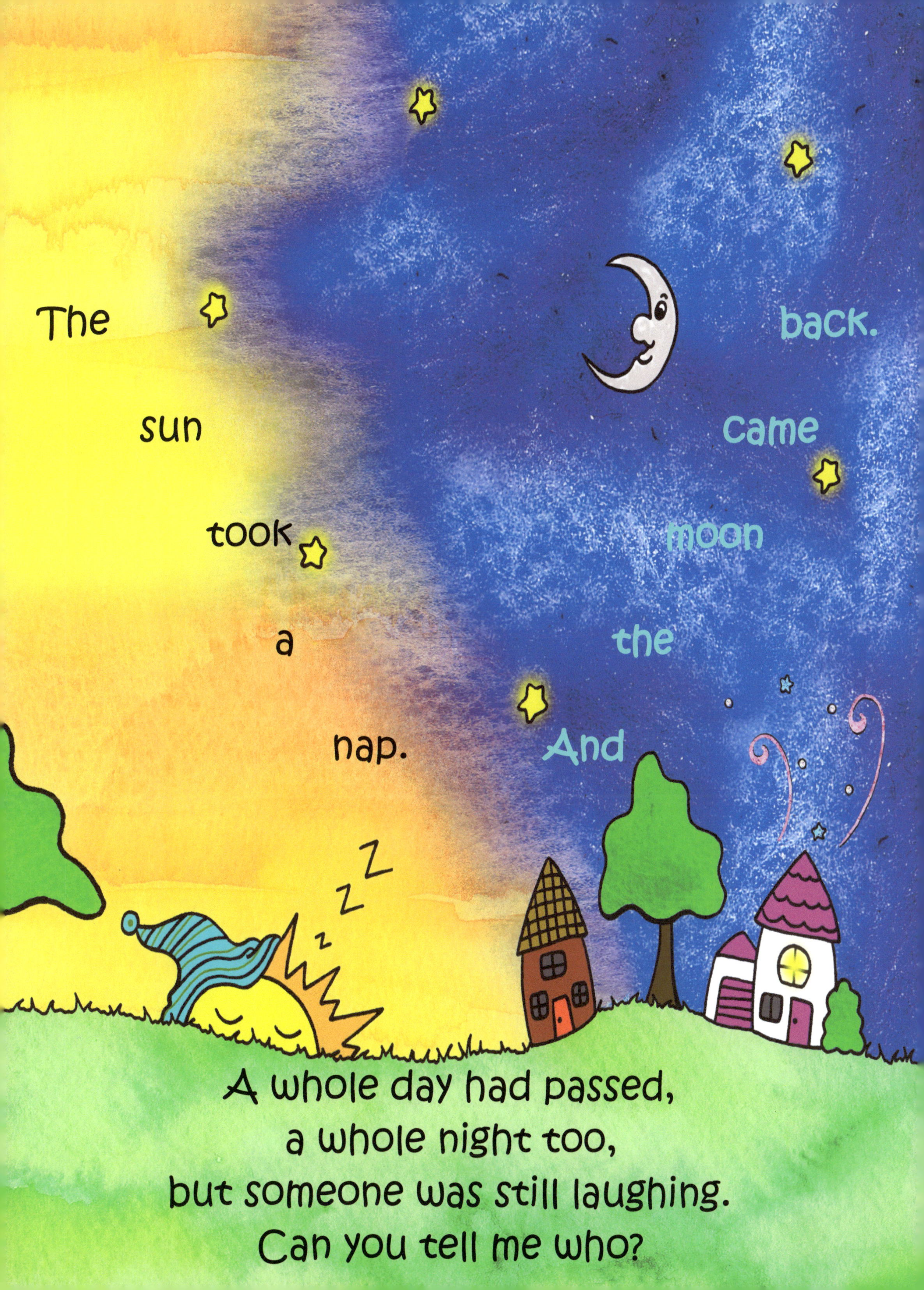

The sun took a nap.

And the moon came back.

A whole day had passed,
a whole night too,
but someone was still laughing.
Can you tell me who?

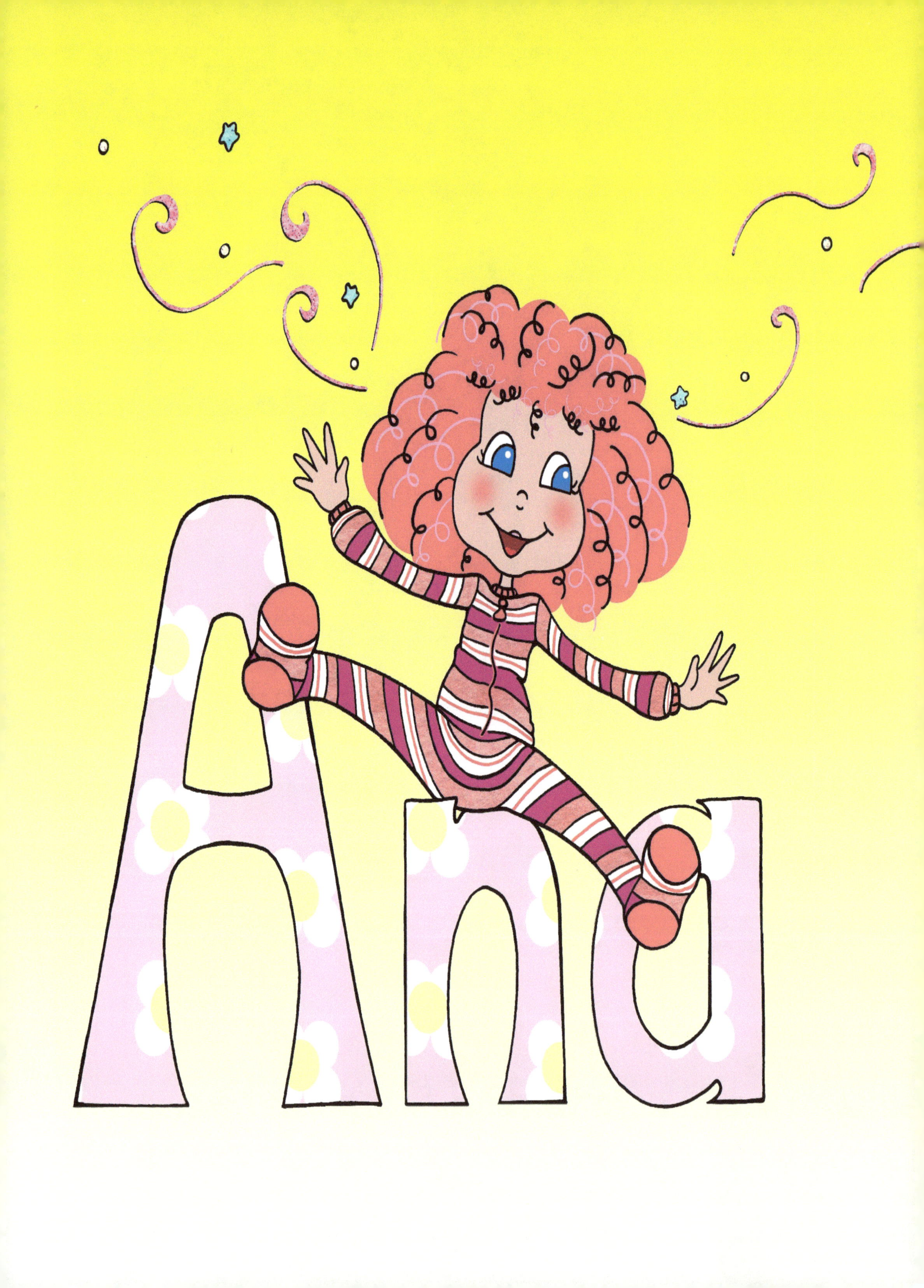
Ana

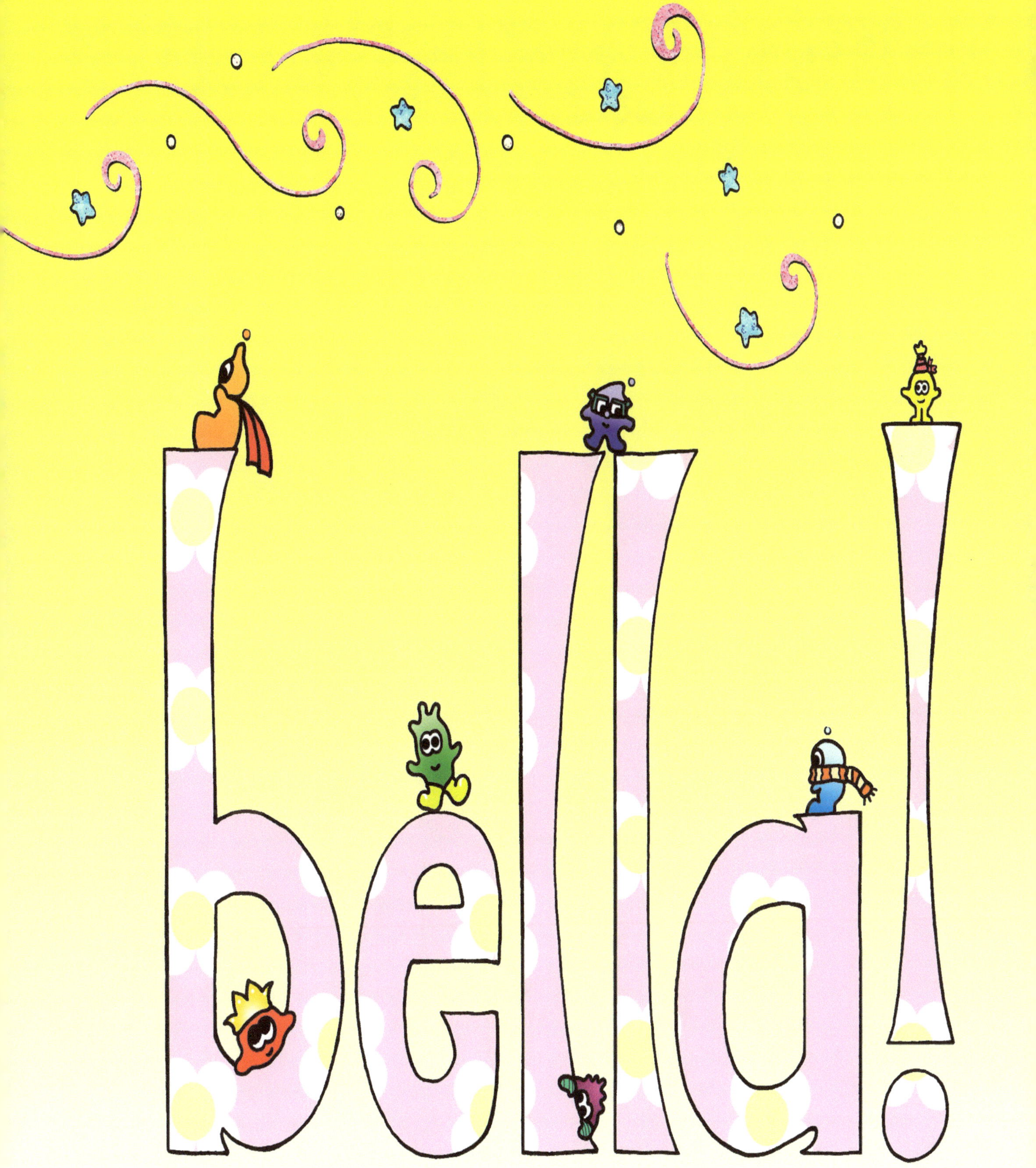
bella!

She was as happy as can be,
giggling and playing with all the silly Rhompees.
She had laughed the whole day
and the whole night away.

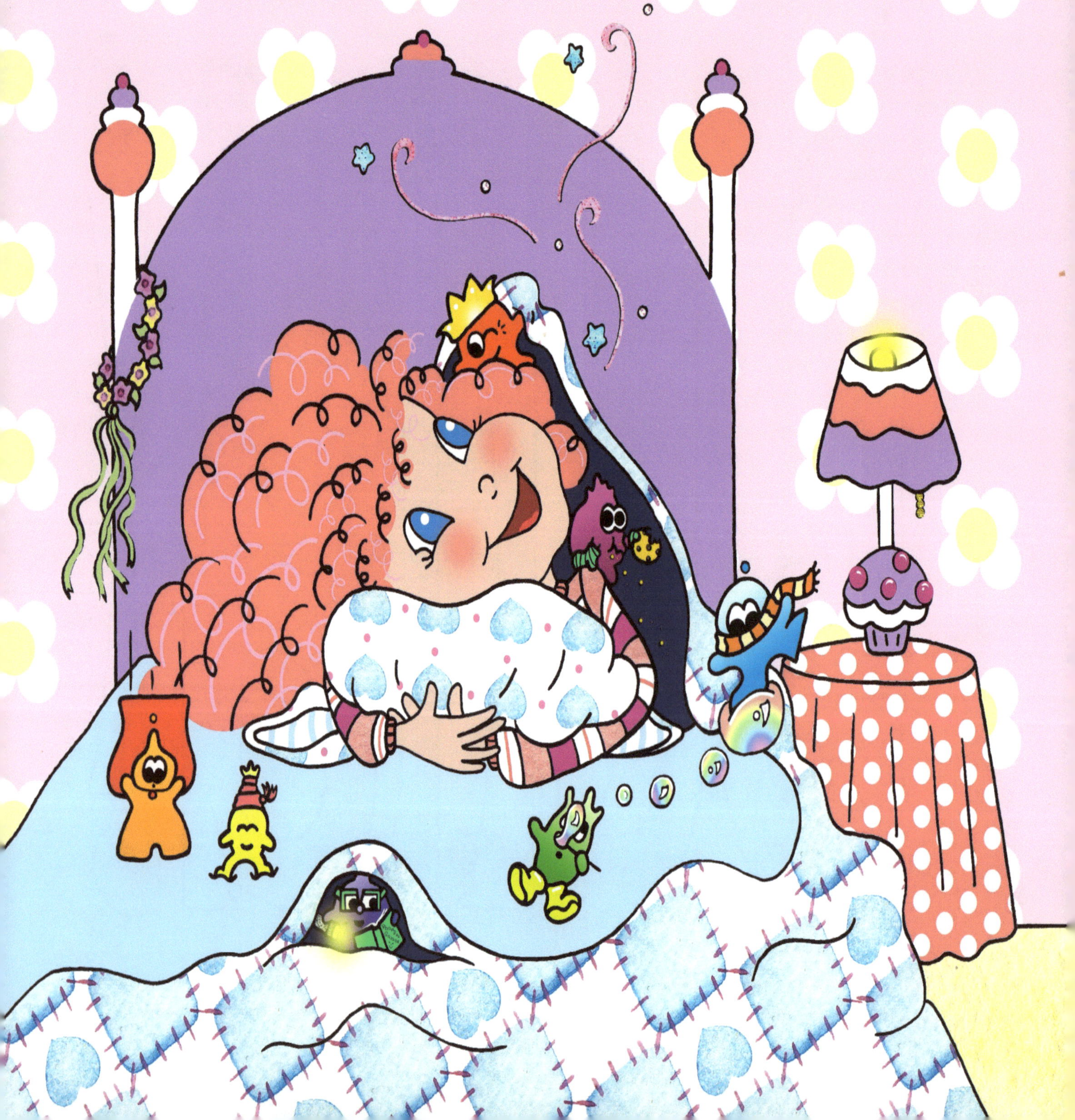

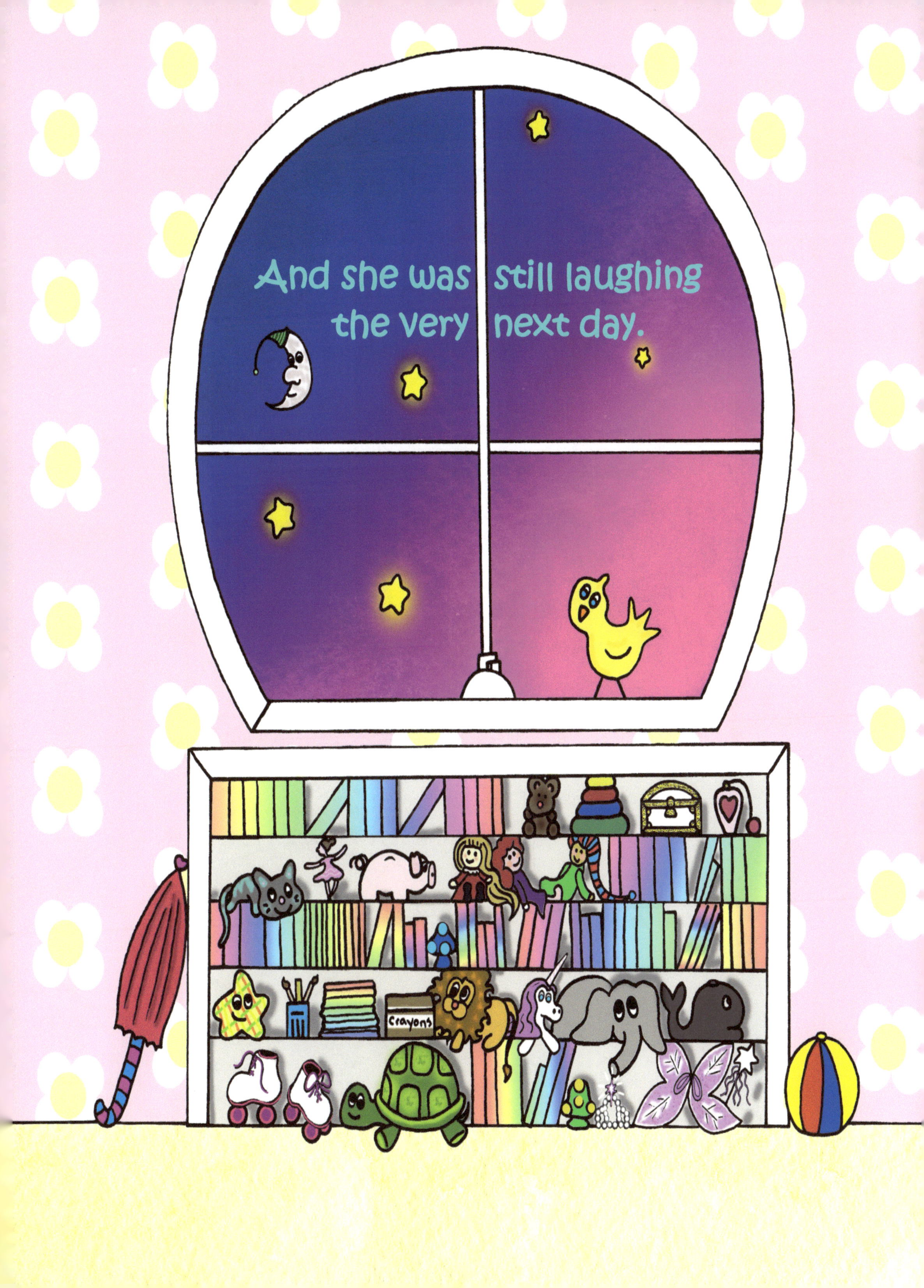
Crayons

And she was still laughing
the very next day.

When her mommy came in
that morning to see
if she was still laughing
or if she was asleep,
she found Anabella
wide awake and said

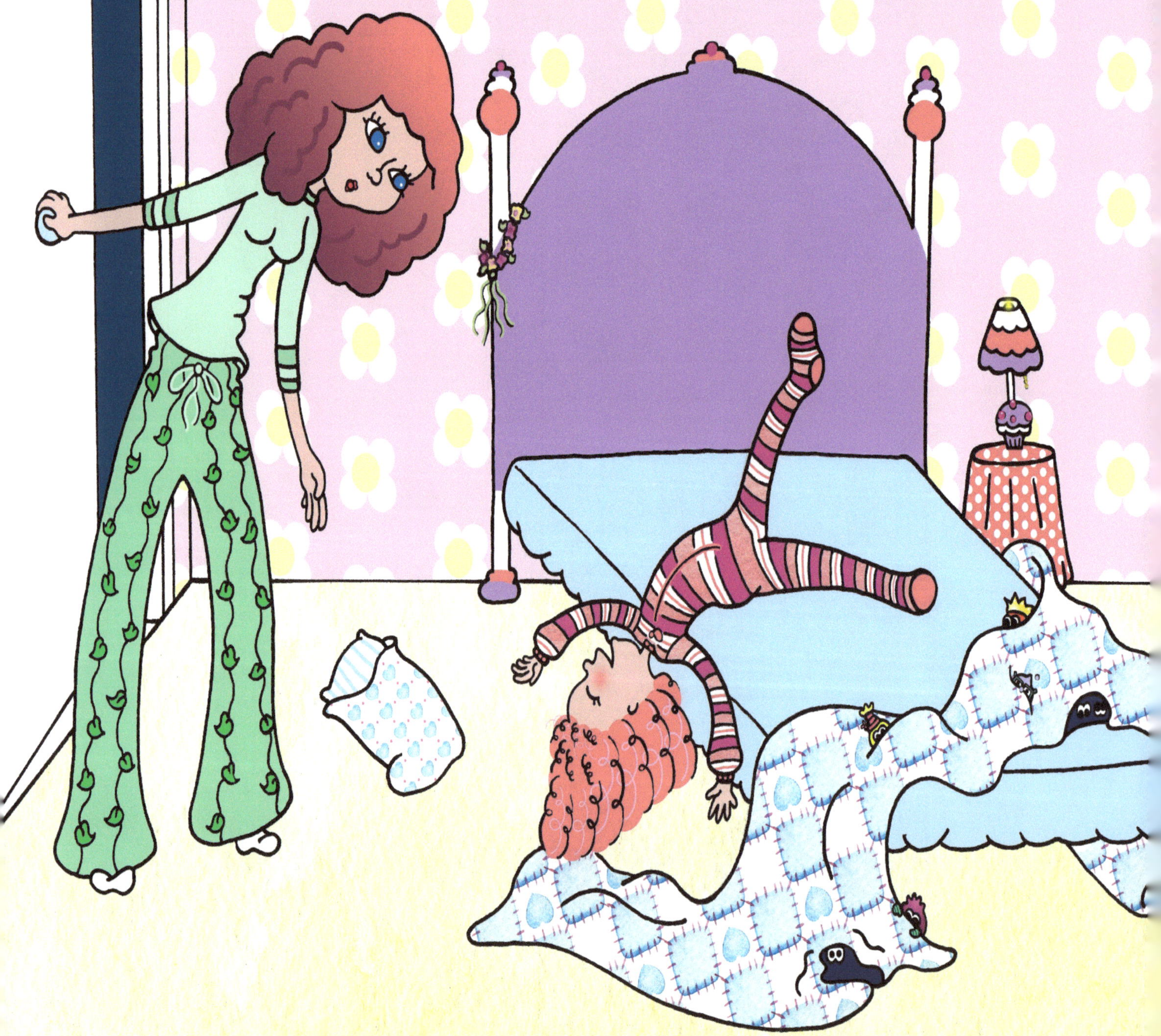

"Did you giggle all night Anabella,
or did you go to bed?"

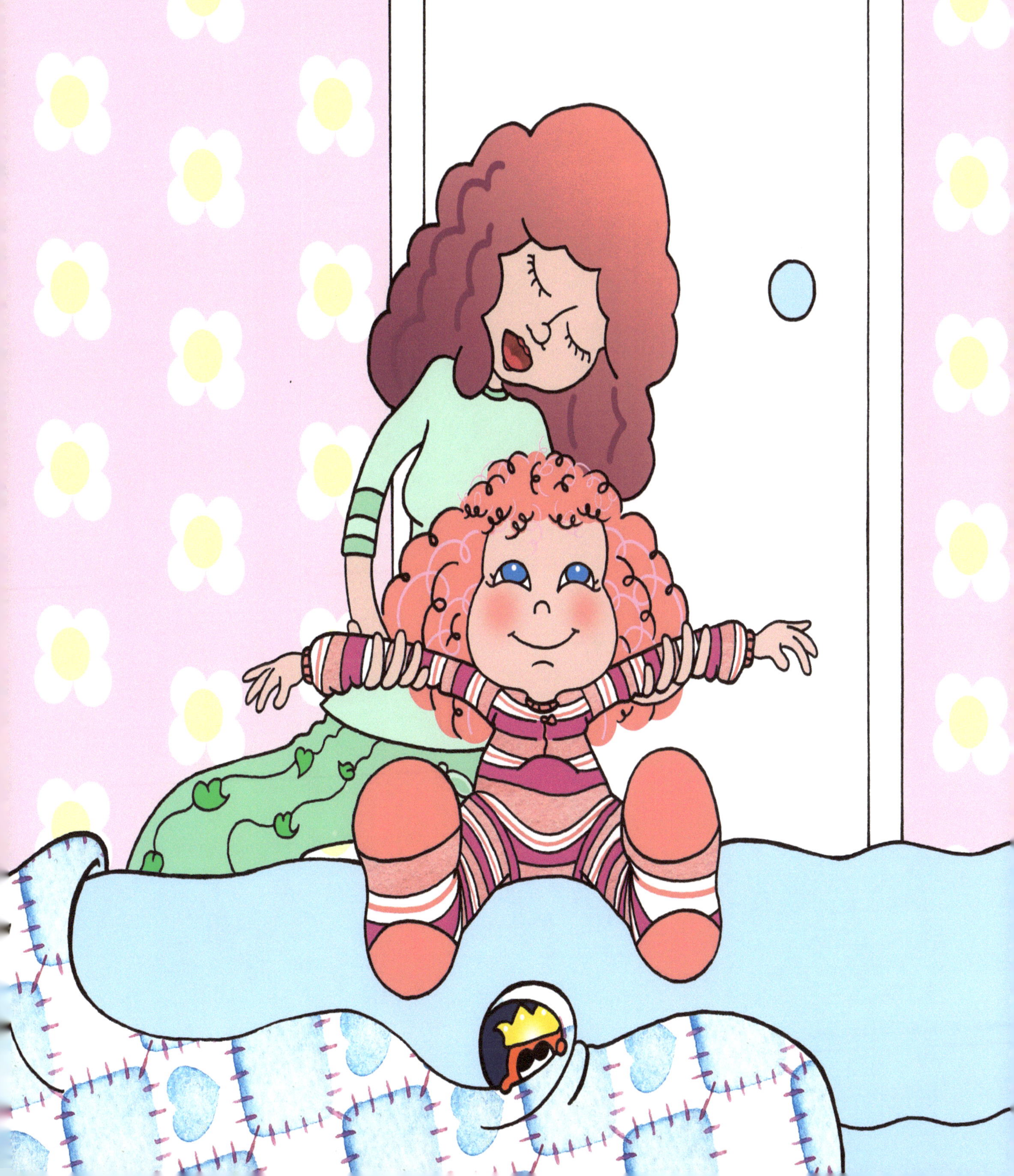

"I giggled all night!"
Anabella said.

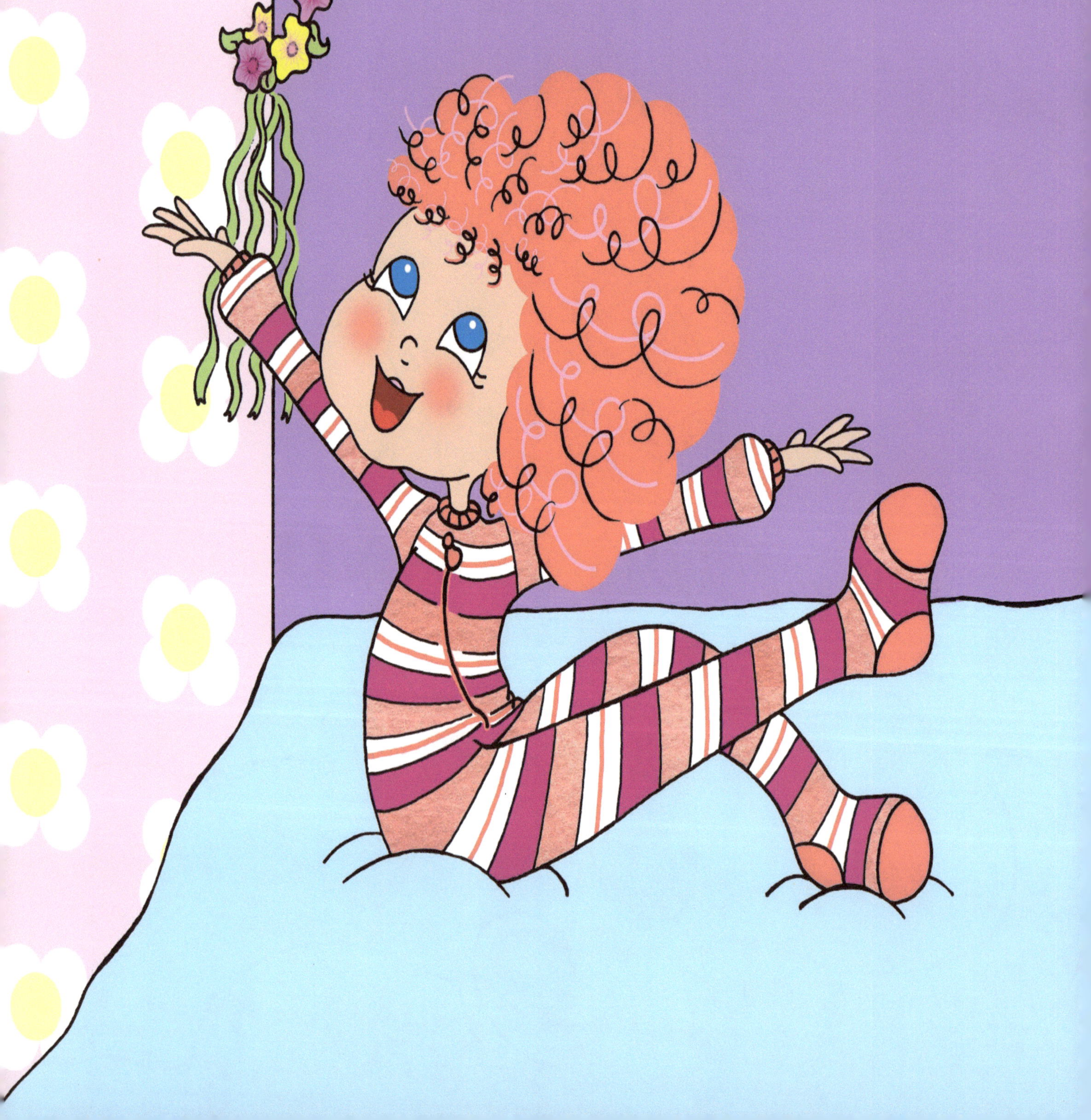

"The Rhompees wouldn't go to sleep and kept playing near my bed."

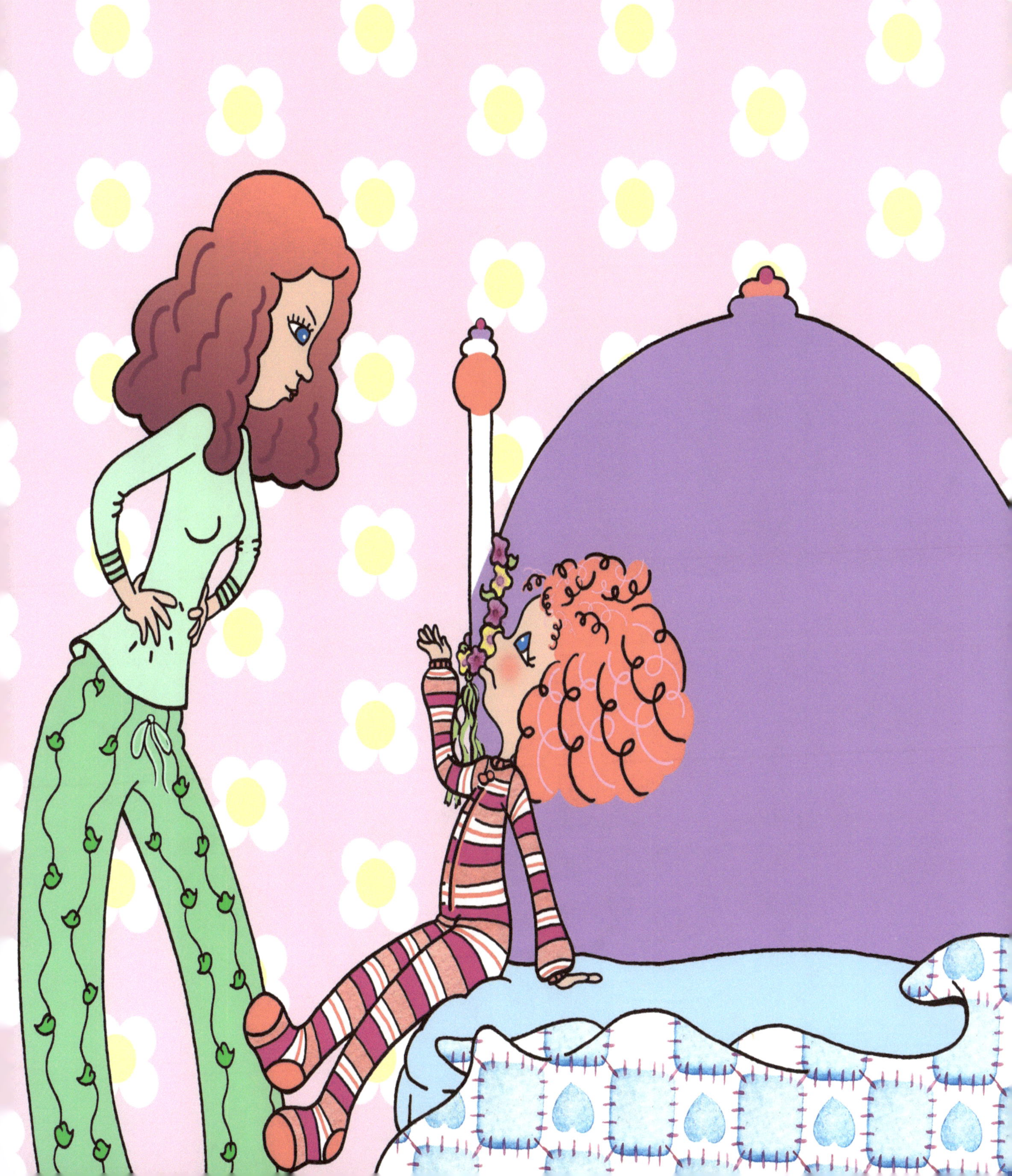

"Uh oh!" Anabella thought
"I hope Mommy isn't mad."

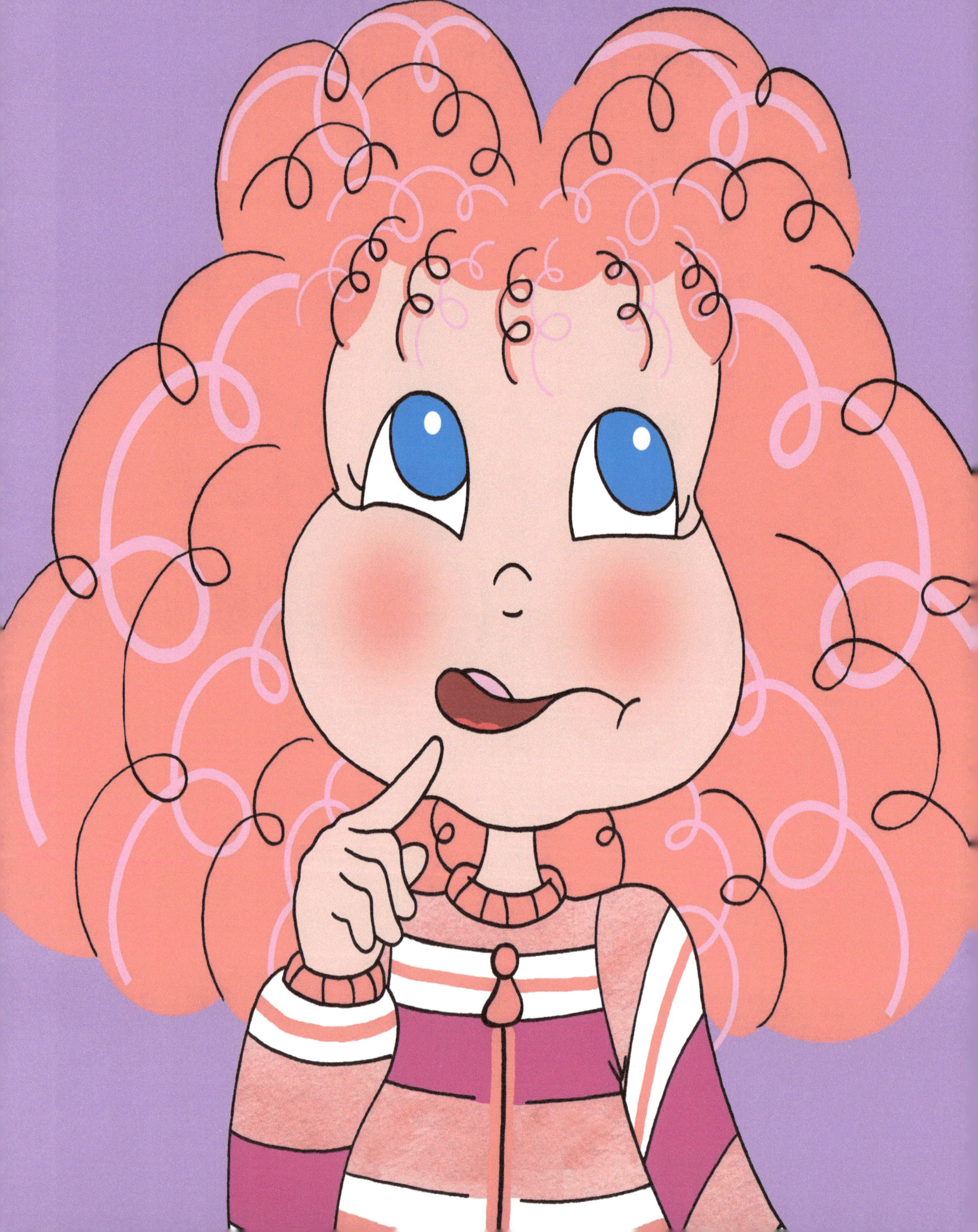

"Anabella" her mommy said,
"Those silly Rhompees were very bad!"

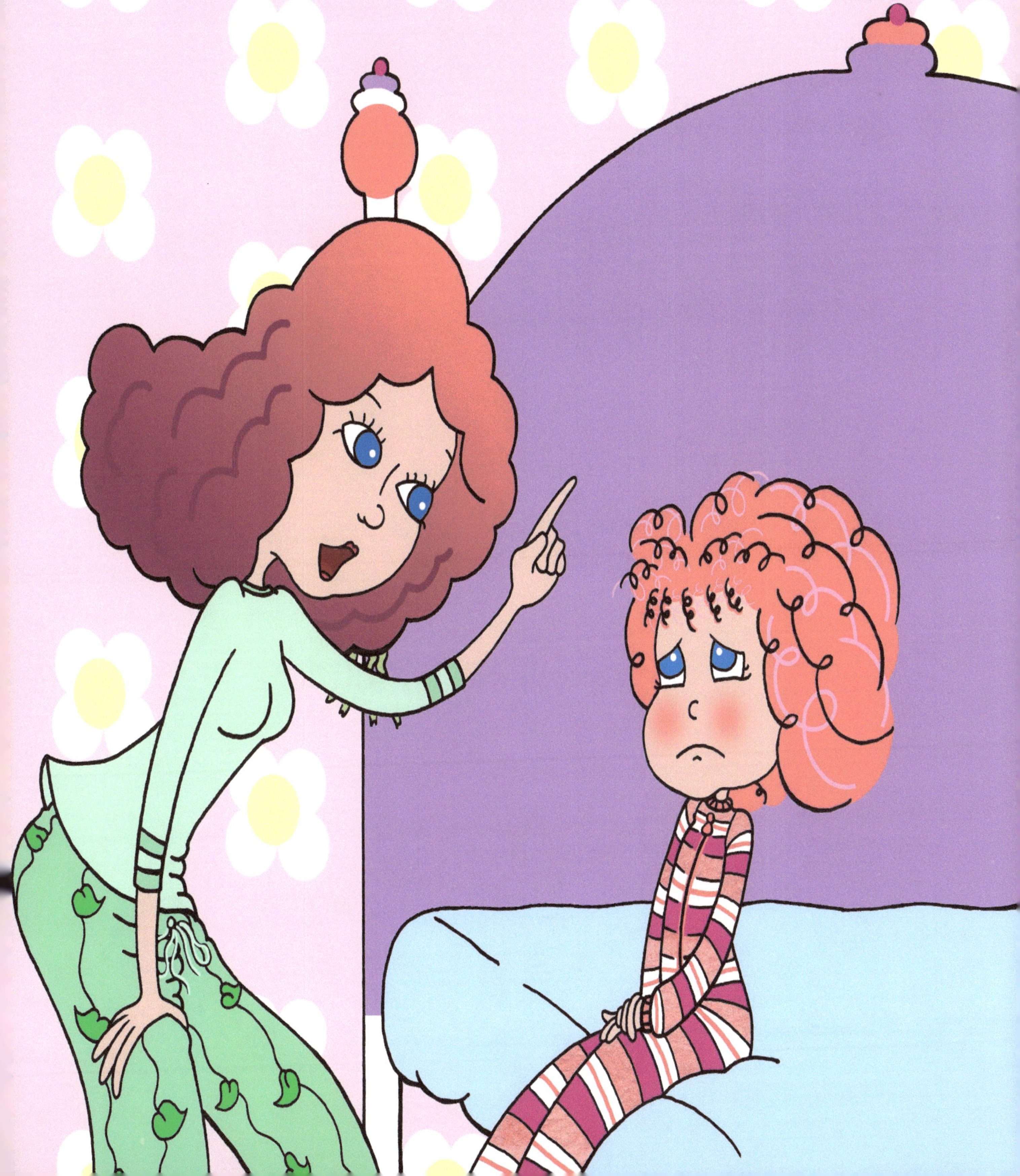

The silly Rhompees had played again and again,

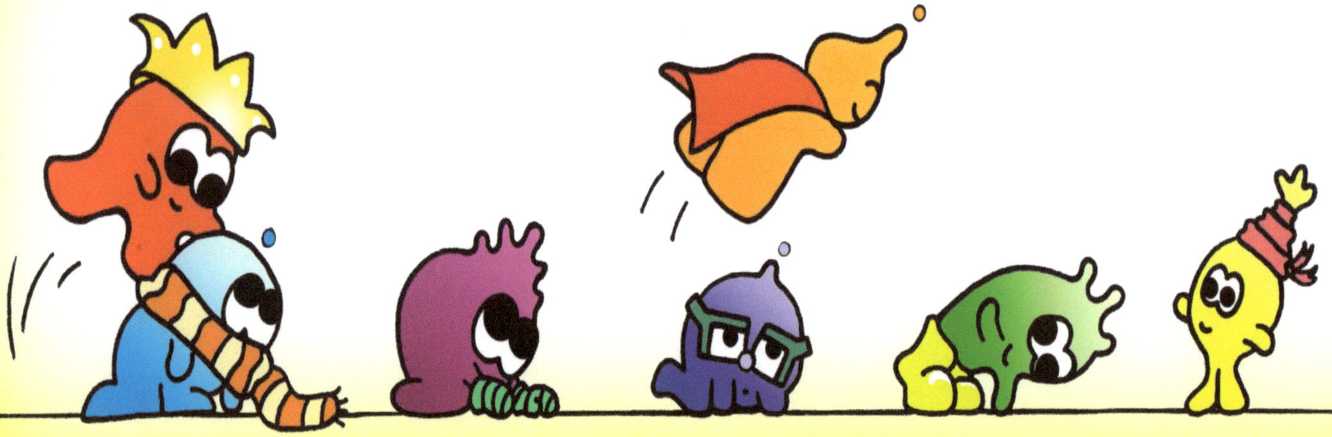

and again,

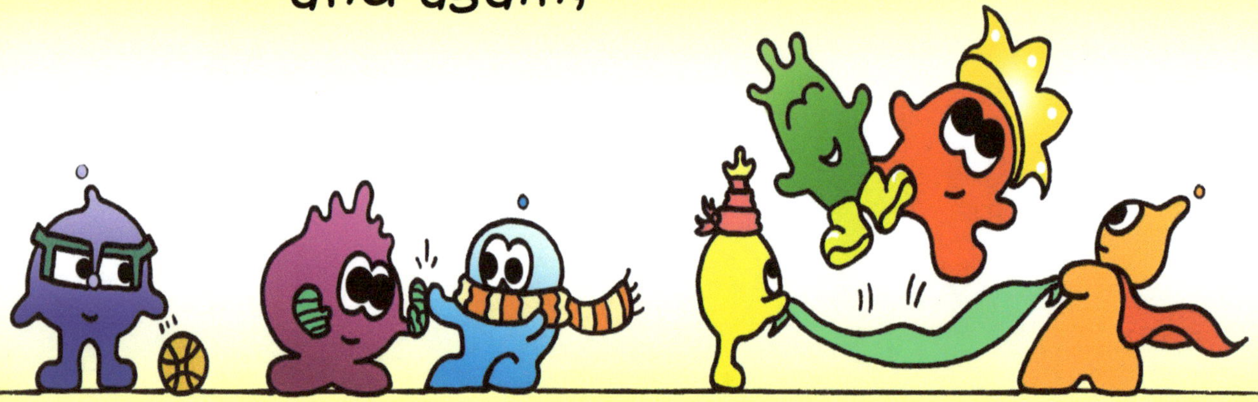

and again!

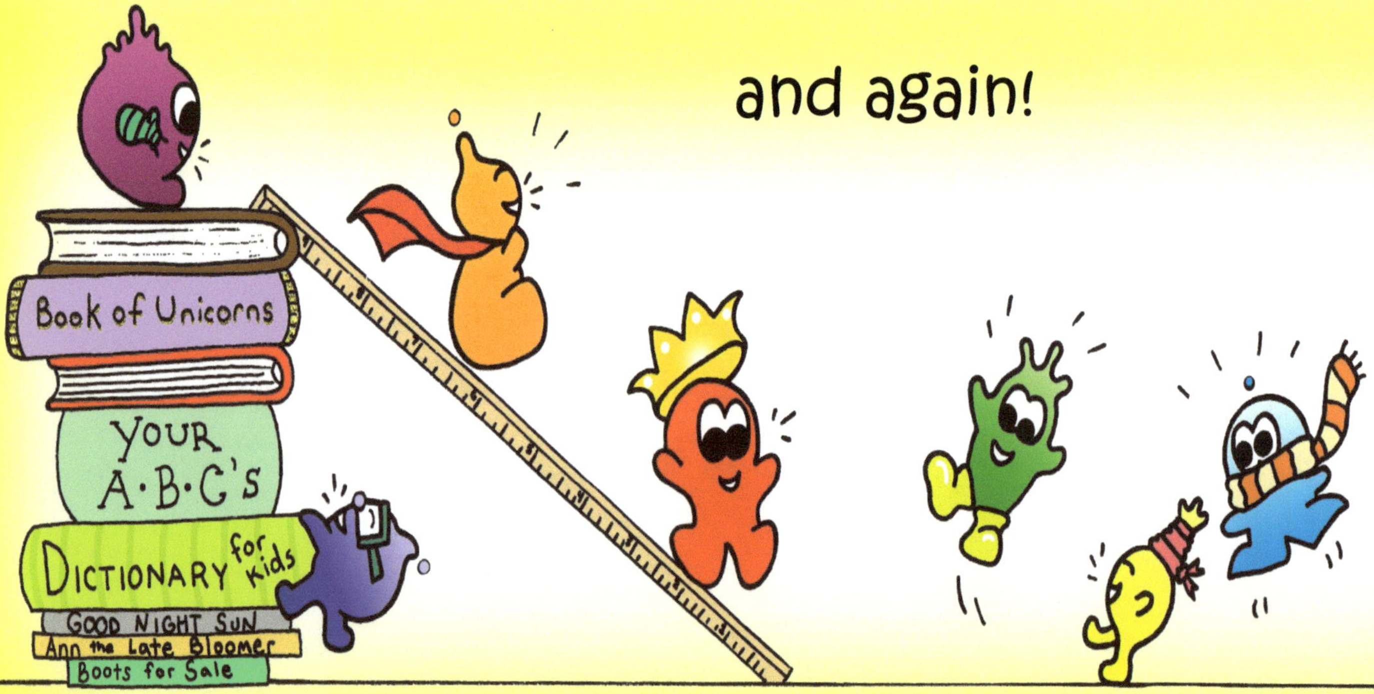
Book of Unicorns
YOUR A·B·C's
DICTIONARY for kids
GOOD NIGHT SUN
Ann the Late Bloomer
Boots for Sale

Now Anabella wanted them to stop.
And she wanted them to listen.

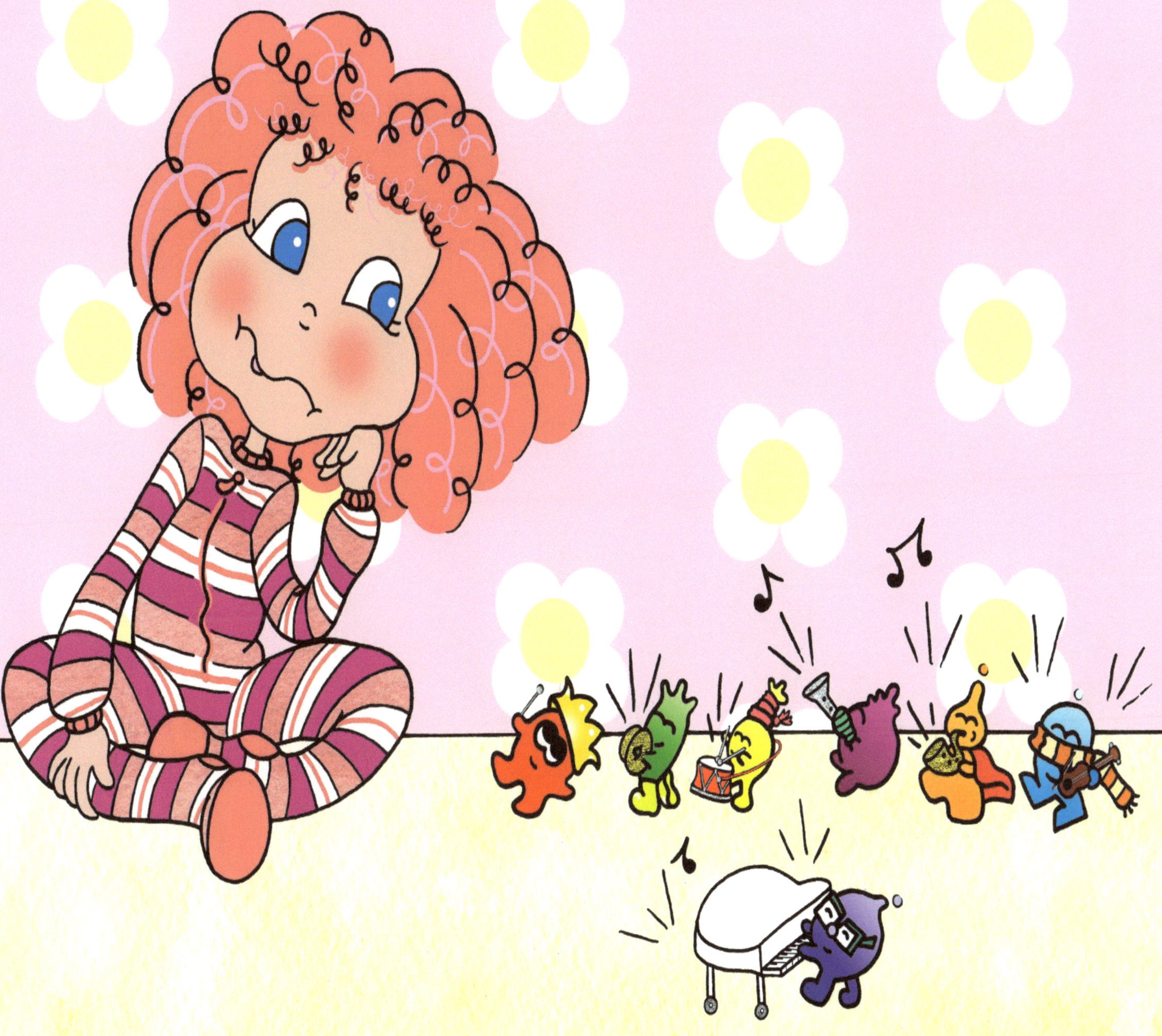

"Wont you guys go to sleep now, pretty please with sugar bees?" Anabella said.

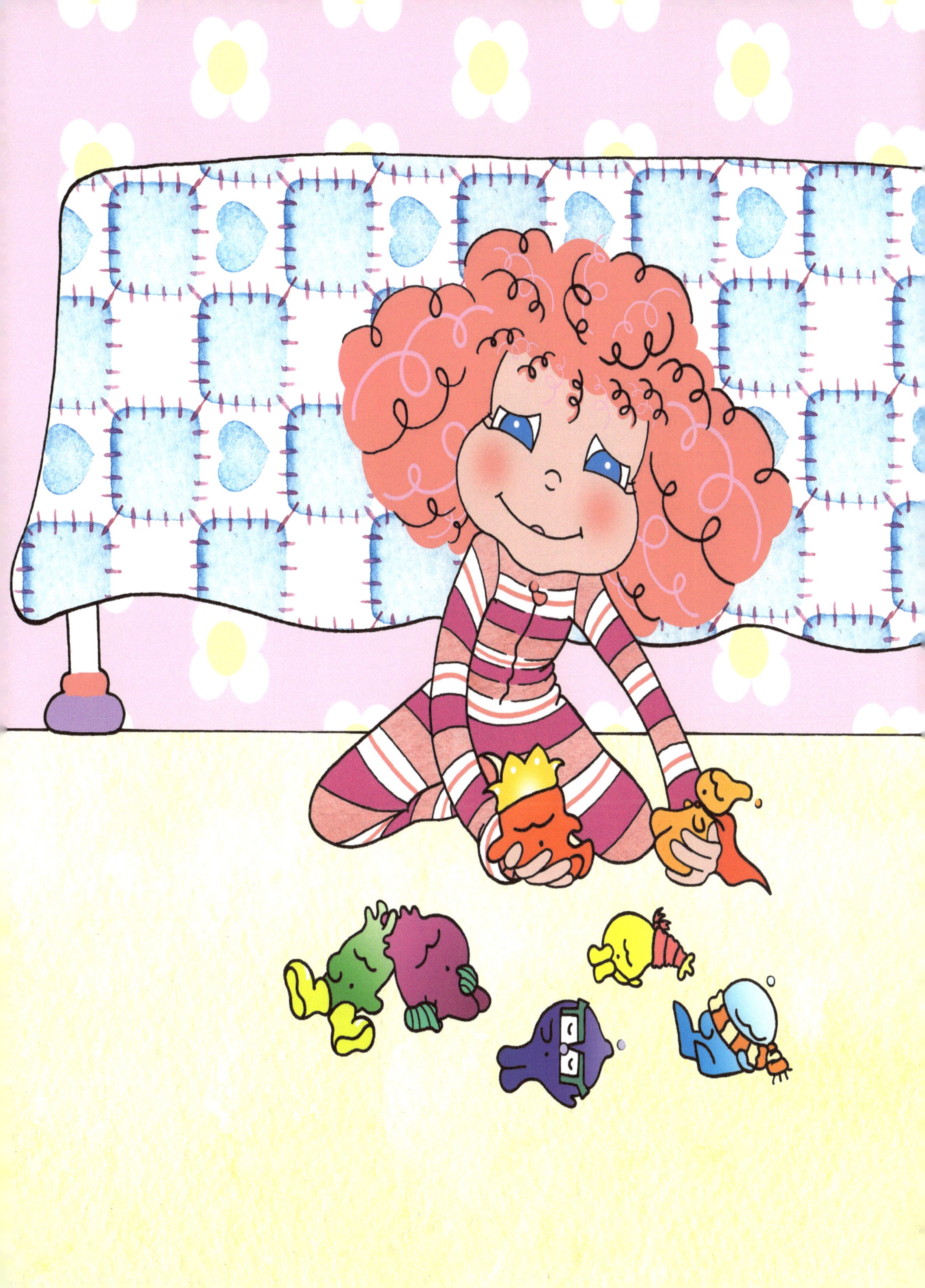

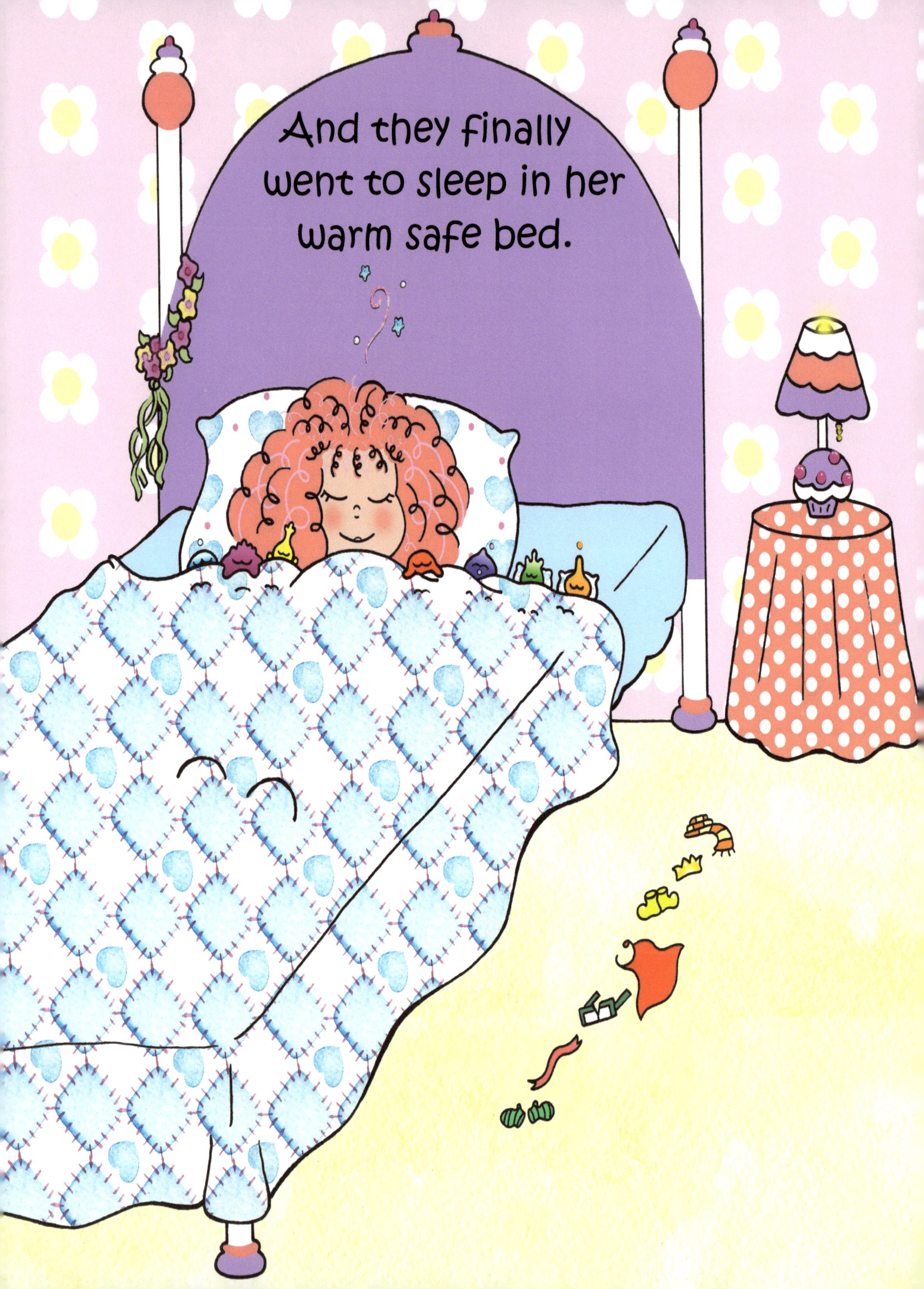
And they finally
went to sleep in her
warm safe bed.

www.ingramcontent.com/pod-product-compliance
Lightning Source LLC
Chambersburg PA
CBHW041238040426
42445CB00004B/77
* 9 7 8 0 9 8 2 8 5 3 5 9 7 *